The Preface to of Virgil (

Joseph Trapp

Alpha Editions

This edition published in 2024

ISBN 9789361471995

Design and Setting By

Alpha Editions
www.alphaedis.com

Email - info@alphaedis.com

As per information held with us this book is in Public Domain.
This book is a reproduction of an important historical work.
Alpha Editions uses the best technology to reproduce historical work
in the same manner it was first published to preserve its original nature.
Any marks or number seen are left intentionally to preserve.

Contents

INTRODUCTION ....- 1 -

NOTES TO THE INTRODUCTION ....- 8 -

BIBLIOGRAPHICAL NOTE ....- 9 -

THE PREFACE. ....- 11 -

FOOTNOTES: ....- 54 -

INTRODUCTION

Joseph Trapp's translation of the *Aeneid* was first published in two volumes dated respectively 1718 and 1720. Its appearance coincided with his vacation of his chair as Professor of Poetry at the University of Oxford, an office which he was the first to hold and to which he had been elected in 1708.[1] The translation may be seen both as a valediction to the University by one whose subsequent career was to be made through the paths of clerical controversy and as a claim for the attention and patronage of the great world. The dedicatee was William, Lord North and Grey, and the list of subscribers is rich with the names of lords temporal and spiritual, including the Lord Primate of Ireland (Thomas Lindsay), who took four sets. Addison, Arbuthnot, Berkeley, Thomas Sheridan, Tickell, Swift, Young, and Thomas Warton (who succeeded Trapp as Professor of Poetry) also subscribed, but not Pope, whose views on Homer, Trapp criticised and misquoted. The University of Oxford was generous in its support (Cambridge was less so). We have, thus, in Trapp's *Aeneid* a translation of Virgil that was probably read by many of the important figures of the English Augustan cultural milieu. In turn, Trapp, writing with highest academic authority, offers in his Preface an important critical account of Virgil's epic.

Trapp's career was typical of his times, combining literary and critical activity with religious and political partisanship. He was born into a clerical family in 1679 (his father was rector of Cherrington, Gloucestershire) and after proceeding to New College School, Oxford, and Wadham College, he attracted the attention of the wits by a series of paraphrases, translations, complimentary effusions (including "Peace. A poem: inscribed to ... Viscount Bolingbroke, 1713"), and at least one successful tragedy, *Abra-Mule; or Love and Empire* (1704). In public affairs he was active in the defence of Henry Sacheverell, and his partisanship here must have cemented his relationship with Dr. William Lancaster, one of the bail for Sacheverell, who was Vice-Chancellor of Oxford at the time of Trapp's election to the chair of poetry. Less fortunate was Trapp's association with the dedicatee of the translation of the *Aeneid*, for Lord North and Grey, who was prominent in seeking to quash Sacheverell's impeachment (and became a privy-councillor in 1711), was committed to the Tower in 1722 for complicity in the Atterbury plot and ended his days a wanderer on the continent. That Atterbury himself was a subscriber to the *Aeneid* serves further to underline Trapp's Tory affiliations. The dedication by Trapp of his Oxford lectures on poetry (*Praelectiones Poeticae*, 1711-19)[2] to

Bolingbroke appears to complete a fatal concatenation of literary and political association in the light of events after the death of Queen Anne.

Nonetheless, Trapp survived and prospered. Under the Tories he had been for a time chaplain to Sir Constantine Phipps, Lord Chancellor of Ireland, and shortly afterwards to Bolingbroke, who stood as godfather to Trapp's son Henry. During the Tory collapse, Peterborough presented him to the rectorship of Dauntsey in Wiltshire; Dr. Lancaster obtained for him the lectureship at St. Martin-in-the-Fields, Westminster; and in the 1730s Bolingbroke, restored, preferred him to the rectorship of Harlington, Middlesex. Other livings and the presidency of Sion College were to accrue for faithful service, as Trapp turned his pen to the defence of the established church: first against the Roman Catholics (for which, perhaps, the University of Oxford created him Doctor of Divinity in 1728) and later against the Methodists, especially in his discourses on *The Nature, Folly, Sin, and Danger of being Righteous over much* (1739).

Such engagements left him little time for literary creativity in the years before his death in 1747. However, Trapp finally finished his labors on Virgil by issuing a translation of the works (1731); and his poem *Thoughts Upon the Four Last Things: Death, Judgment, Heaven, Hell* (1734-35) shows him attempting to combine literary pleasure with theological instruction—a potent mixture forcibly administered to his parishoners, for it is recorded that he desired in his will that a copy be presented to each "housekeeper" among them. *The Paradisus Amissus, Latine Redditus* appeared in 1741-44. This translation of Milton into Latin is more than a freak of the neoclassical mind. It is the natural complement to his earlier translation of the *Aeneid* into Miltonic blank verse as well as his attempt to judge the classic sublime by the achievement of the masterwork of Christian epic, a task that had preoccupied him as Oxford's Professor of Poetry.

The importance of Trapp's Preface to his version of the *Aeneid* (and the extensive notes to the text) lies fundamentally in the fusion of Miltonic example with neoclassical precept in an attempt both to understand the Latin text rationally and to communicate the intensely exciting and moving experience that the *Aeneid* evokes. This was a new departure. French Aristotelian criticism of classical epic was (inevitably) not influenced by Milton. In the English tradition, neither Dryden in his Dedication of the *Aeneid* nor Pope in the prefatory material to the *Iliad* (with which Trapp frequently takes issue) used *Paradise Lost* as the basic touchstone of value. Trapp was to be sneered at in Delany's "News from Parnassus" for claiming in Pythagorean vein that the spirit of Milton had descended to him. This was unfair; he made no such claim. Trapp was trying to discover affinities between past and present in poetic sensibility and in the use of language. In doing so, he sought to place a major English poet in relation to

Virgil, and he judged from this example that the English blank verse line had more of the grandeur of the Latin hexameter than the couplet in the hands even of Dryden or Pope. His taste told him that the imaginative invention and force of Milton had more of the Virgilian spirit than the elegant correctness of English Augustanism. He argues his position with vigor in the Preface and in his notes, and often with illustrative example.

The conventional view that Trapp wished to change by the interpolation of Milton was that, whereas Virgil merited the laurel for judgment and decorum, Homer possessed greater "fire," "sublimity," "fecundity," "majesty," and "vastness" (to use Trapp's terms). Homer was praised as the great original and inventor; Virgil followed in his steps with more refinement and rationality, showing everywhere that good sense and polished concision of expression characteristic of the Augustan age (so, for instance, René Rapin claimed in the well-known *Comparaison*).[3] One blossomed with the wild abundance and grandeur of nature; the other displayed that cultivated order shown in fields and gardens. Trapp accepts all that was granted to the Roman poet, but he claims for Virgil, Homeric qualities also: his borrowings are merely the basis for his invention (witness the tale of Dido); and as for the fire of sublimity, Trapp, like a critical Prometheus, filches that also. Among the many instances of the Virgilian fire given in the Preface, he cites "the Arrival of *Aeneas* with his Fleet and Forces" in the tenth book. His translation runs thus:

> Amaz'd stood *Turnus*, and th' *Ausonian* Chiefs;
> 'Till, looking back, they saw the Navy move
> Cov'ring the Sea, and gliding make to Shore.
> Fierce burns his Helm; and from his tow'ring Crest
> Flame flashes; and his Shield's round Bossy Gold
> Vomits vast Fires: As when in gloomy Night
> Ensanguin'd Comets shoot a dismal Glare;
> Or the red Dog-Star, rising on the World,
> To wretched Mortals threatens Dearth, and Plagues,
> With Baleful Light; and saddens all the Sky.(360 *ff.*)

Trapp does not play the trite old game of setting the texts of Homer and Virgil in comparison, but what comes to his mind at once in his note, and rightly, given the language of his translation, is Milton describing Satan:

> Like a Comet burn'd,
> That fires the Length of *Ophiucus* huge
> In th' Artick Sky; and from his horrid hair
> Shakes Pestilence and War.(II. 708-711)

Similarly, when Aeneas hastens to meet Turnus in the twelfth book, Miltonic translation and Miltonic original are brought together to show the similarity between Virgilian and Christian sublime:

Aeneas ... with Joy
Exults; and thunders terrible in Arms.
As great as *Athos*, or as *Eryx* great,
Or Father *Apennine*, when crown'd with Okes
He waves the ruffled Forest on his Brow,
And rears his snowy Summit to the Clouds.(902 ff.)

On th' other Side *Satan* allarm'd
Collecting all his Might, dilated stood;
Like *Teneriff*, or *Atlas* unremov'd:
His Stature reach'd the Sky, and on his Crest
Sat Horrour plum'd.(IV. 985-989)

In the light of such illustration, it is not surprising that Trapp, in the Preface, when he wishes to give the feel of the Virgilian sublime, quotes Milton's description of the creation:

Let there be Light, said God; and forthwith Light
Ethereal, first of Things, Quintessence pure,
Sprang from the Deep.(p. xxx)

When he wants to show what grandeur with propriety the English language can achieve (even in the teeth of Dryden's rendering of Virgil, which he pertinently censures), he chooses his prime examples from Milton: witness the account of Satan "Hurl'd headlong, flaming from th' ethereal Sky...." It was a bold undertaking by Trapp, for Pope's version of Homer, elegantly correct in couplets, was in the press. Many a man was to suffer more in *The Dunciad* for less.[4]

Trapp's immediate critical associates in England clearly are John Dennis and Joseph Addison, and the origins of Trapp's thinking in classical antiquity may be found in Longinus. Dennis had united Milton with the poets of antiquity as an example of the passionate effects of the religious sublime,[5] while Addison (who had already translated a fragment of *Aeneid* III into blank verse) in his *Spectator* papers on *Paradise Lost* had tastefully combined the structural formalism of Aristotelian criticism of the epic with enthusiastic comment on the grandeur and beauty of Milton's verse. To these must be added Trapp's favorite, Roscommon, who in *An Essay on Translated Verse* (1685)[6] had interposed an imitation of Milton to illustrate how English verses might rise to Roman greatness. But it would be unfair to Trapp merely to reduce him to a series of component sources. He adopts and adapts; and as far as the criticism of Virgil was concerned, his Preface and his notes are a refreshing plea for something that he felt had not been sufficiently emphasized in the *Aeneid*: the ever-varying energetic passion that Longinian criticism had claimed was an essential quality of the greatest literary works. Trapp's choice of Miltonic example is only one means by which he emphasises that to truly respond to the *Aeneid* (as to any major poem) was to be ravished by an overwhelming emotive experience. "The Art, and Triumph of Poetry are in nothing more seen, and felt, than in *Moving the Passions*," he comments in his "Remarks" on the tragical action of the fourth book to which he prefaced "*An Essay upon the Nature, and Art of Moving the Passions in Tragedy, and Epic Poetry*" (I. 377). "A Man cannot command his own Motions, while he reads This; The very *Verses are alive*" (II. 942) is a typical comment from his "Remarks" (on breaking the truce in the twelfth book). He introduces the third book by citing Horace: the poet's art is like magic, transporting us now to Thebes, now to Athens (I. 365). Sometimes he throws up his hands in rapture at the *je ne sais quoi*: "Some Beauties are the more so, for not being capable of Explanation. I feel it, tho' I cannot account for it" (I. 339). It is to the text the Preface lays the foundation for this kind of response in its emphasis on the emotive range of Virgil—on his power to burn and to freeze, to raise admiration, terror, and pity. "The *Greek* Poet knew little of the Passions, in comparison of the *Roman*" his argument runs, setting Virgil on the peak of Parnassus.

This enthusiastic excitement is firmly controlled in the Preface by the disciplines of more formal criticism, and here, inevitably, Trapp follows the same kind of standard authorities as Dryden in his translation. It would be untypical of the man not to give positive guarantees of his learning and respectability. He shows that he had absorbed the arguments of René le Bossu's *Traité du Poème Epique* (1675) and knows Jean Regnauld de Segrais' translation of the *Aeneid* (1668). He was familiar with René Rapin's *Réflexions sur la Poétique d'Aristote* (1674) and André Dacier's *La Poétique d'Aristote Traduite en Français. Avec des Remarques* (1692). The name of J. C. Scaliger intrudes, if only to be mentioned with distaste; for the pedantic querulousness of Scaliger's extended comparison of Homer with Virgil attracted Trapp no more than it did Addison, both critics, in the English humanistic tradition, being more concerned with an appreciative and elegant brevity than with exhaustive scholarship. It was necessary also to show some knowledge of the quarrel of the ancients and moderns; but Trapp is concerned with the integrity of European culture, not with the inane counting of points for or against past or present and not at all with scoring off personal antagonists. In comparison, he makes Swift, who always sneered at him, and even Pope seem sometimes trivial and bitchy.

The restrained humanism of the Preface is noticeable. Thus, although the critical concerns of the age lead Trapp to seek to annex "clear Ideas" "to the Words, *Action, Fable, Incident*, and *Episode*," there is nothing in his writing resembling the prolegomena to the *Aeneid* in the Delphin edition,[7] prolegomena that define epic from the doctrine of Aristotle as the imitation of one action, illustrious, complete, of a certain magnitude, which by narration in hexameter verse raises eminent men to the prime virtues by delight and admiration, proceeds to define the *actio, fabula, mores, sententia*, and *dictio* in the abstract, and then demonstrates that the definitions fit the *Aeneid* (*ergo* it is an epic poem). This is scientific method ossified. On the other hand, if one compares Dryden's Dedication of the *Aeneid*, Trapp equally eschews the quirky digressiveness (and the wholesale borrowings), which give to Dryden's writing both its sense of personal and spontaneous insight and yet its prolixity and mere messiness. Trapp had studied the art to blot. The reader is spared Dryden's extended and pointless discussion (at second hand) of how long the action of the *Aeneid* takes, let alone whether this is the right length for an epic action or whether Aeneas was too lacrymose to be a hero (presumably Trapp thought that those who will believe that will believe anything). Likewise, Dryden's political insights, gathered as much from his own experience as from Roman history, are also swiftly passed by for more aesthetic concerns. Perhaps the view of Dryden (and Pope) that the *Aeneid* was a party piece like *Absalom and Achitophel* was unbalanced,[8] but Trapp might have reflected that, if any man knew about political poetry, it was John Dryden and that the *Aeneid* has a place in the history of the Roman civil wars. But the Oxford professor was more concerned with the sublime and beautiful.

As a critic of classical epic there can be little reasonable doubt that Trapp stands comparison with either Dryden or Pope, and the honesty and value of his critical endeavor are worth respect. He can be cool and analytical when dispassionate reason is required (witness his account of how in brevity and morality Virgil surpasses Homer); but he is in no sense tied by a rigidly formalistic approach, happy to praise even that "*Variety*" which "justifies the Breach of almost any Rule" (Preface p. xlvi), or the organic development of structure that seems to be "*no Method* at all" (II. 953). Essentially, behind this firm but flexible criticism, there is a compelling sense that to read a great poem is to submit to an overwhelming experience; and his criticism is always hastening to illustration, with the tacit appeal, "It is like this, isn't it?" What is particularly stimulating, whether one accepts the claim or not that Virgilian style and sensibility are reflected in Milton, is the continual illumination of the classics by the vernacular and particularly by modern example. It seems as if he is claiming that, to understand the past, we must respond to the literature of our own culture and that there are no important barriers between antiquity and the modern world, the appreciation of foreign languages and our own tongue. All true culture is always immediate and felt vitally as part of our being. In attempting to express this, Trapp is in touch with what is best in neoclassicism.

University of Reading.

NOTES TO THE INTRODUCTION

[1] He had held the chair for the maximum period of ten years permitted by the original statute. For further particulars, see Thomas Hearne, *Remarks and Collections*, ed. C. E. Doble (Oxford, 1886), entries for 14 July and 27 July 1708.

[2] There is a translation by William Bowyer, assisted by William Clarke, entitled *Lectures on Poetry* (London, 1742).

[3] *Comparaison des poèmes d'Homère et de Virgile* (Paris, ?1688).

[4] He is identified by the Twickenham editor as the "*T—*" of the line "*T—s* and T—the church and state gave o'er," in *The Dunciad* of 1728 II. 381, but was dropped from the *Variorum* in 1729. In the Warburton note of 1743, I.33, he may be alluded to in the gibe at "Professors."

[5] Notably in *The Advancement and Reformation of Modern Poetry* (London, 1701) and *The Grounds of Criticism in Poetry* (London, 1704).

[6] The Miltonic passage was added to the second edition (1685). The poem originally appeared the previous year.

[7] Ed. Carolus Ruaeus, i.e. Charles de la Rue (Paris, 1675).

[8] I have further discussed this point in "What God, What Mortal? The *Aeneid* and English Mock-Heroic," *Arion* 8 (1969), 359-79.

BIBLIOGRAPHICAL NOTE

The Preface to Joseph Trapp's translation of *The ÆNEIS of Virgil*, Volume I (1718) is reproduced from a copy of the first edition in the William Andrews Clark Memorial Library (Shelf Mark: *FPR3736/T715V3/1718). A typical type-page (p. vii) measures 231 x 156 mm.

THE ÆNEIS OF VIRGIL,

TRANSLATED INTO

BLANK VERSE:

By *JOSEPH TRAPP*, M. A.

Professor of Poetry in the University of *Oxford*.

-----*Parnaffia Laurus*
Parva sub ingenti Matris se subjicit umbra.
Virg.

VOLUME *the* FIRST.

LONDON:
Printed in the Year MDCCXVIII.

THE PREFACE.

However Poetry may have been dishonoured by the *Follies* of some, and the *Vices* of others; the Abuse, or Corruption of the best Things being always the worst: It will, notwithstanding, be ever regarded, as it ever has been, by the wisest, and most judicious of Men, as the very *Flower* of human *Thinking*, the most *exquisite Spirit* that can be extracted from the *Wit* and *Learning* of Mankind. But I shall not now enter into a formal Vindication of this Divine Art from the many groundless Aspersions which have been cast upon it by Ignorance, and Ill-nature; nor display either it's Dignity in it self, or it's Usefulness both in Philosophy, and Religion; or the delightful Elegancy of it's refined Ideas, and harmonious Expressions. This I have in some measure attempted in another[1] Treatise; to which I rather chuse to refer the Reader, than to repeat what I have already said, tho' in a different Language from This, in which I am now writing. I shall therefore only observe at present, that to hate, or despise Poetry, not only argues a Man deficient in Wisdom, and Learning; but even brings his Virtue and Goodness under Suspicion: What our *Shakespear* says of another melodious Science, being altogether as applicable to This; and Poetry it self being the Musick of Thoughts, and Words, as Musick is the Poetry of Sounds.

The Man that hath not Musick in his Soul,
And is not mov'd with Concord of sweet Sounds;
Is fit for Treasons, Stratagems, and Spoils;
The Motions of his Spirit are dull as Night,
And his Affections dark as Erebus:
Let no such Man be trusted.———[2]

And as Poetry was by the Heathen stiled the *Language of the Gods*; much the same may be said by a Christian of the one true Deity: Since a great part of the Holy Scriptures themselves is to the last degree Poetical, both in Sentiments, and Diction.

But among all the Species, or Kinds of Poetry; That which is distinguished by the Name of Epic, or Heroic, is beyond comparison the Noblest, and most Excellent. *An Heroic Poem, truly such, is undoubtedly the greatest Work which the Soul of Man is capable to perform.* These are the first Words of Mr. *Dryden*'s admirable Dedication of his *English Æneis* to the present Duke of *Buckingham*. They are translated indeed from Monsieur *Rapin*; and are likewise the first Words of his Comparison between *Homer* and *Virgil*.[3] "The Design of it (continues Mr. *Dryden*) is to form the Mind to Heroic

Virtue by Example; 'Tis convey'd in Verse, that it may delight, while it instructs; The Action of it is always One, Entire, and Great. The least, and most trivial Episodes, or Under-Actions, which are interwoven in it, are Parts either necessary, or convenient; that no others can be imagined more suitable to the place in which they are. There is Nothing to be left void in a firm Building; even the Cavities ought not to be filled with Rubbish, which is of a perishable Kind, destructive of the Strength: But with Brick, or Stone, tho' of less pieces, yet of the same Nature, and fitted to the Cranies. Even the least Portions of them must be of the Epic kind; All Things must be Grave, Majestical, and Sublime: Nothing of a foreign Nature, like the trifling Novels, which *Ariosto*,[4] and others have inserted in their Poems. By which the Reader is misled into another sort of Pleasure, opposite to That which is designed in an Epic Poem. One raises the Soul, and hardens it to Virtue; the other softens it again, and unbends it into Vice." But what makes this Kind of Poem preferable to all others, is, that it virtually contains and involves them: I mean their Excellencies and Perfections, besides That which is proper, and peculiar to it self. This likewise is observed by Mr. *Rapin* in the place above-cited: And by this Assertion I do not contradict what I have cited from Mr. *Dryden*; which I am supposed to approve, while I transcribe it. For besides that he does not speak, as I do, of the different *Turns*, and *Modifications* of *Thinking*, and *Writing*, but of *trifling Episodes*, or *Under-Actions*, which he says are improper for this sort of Poetry, and in which I entirely agree with him; I say, besides This, I do not affirm that an Ode, or an Elegy, for example, can with propriety be *actually*, and *formally* inserted in an Heroic Poem; But only that the regular Luxuriancy, and noble Excursions of *That*, and the pathetical and tender Complainings of *This*, are not always forreign to the Nature of an Epic Subject, but are sometimes very properly introduced to adorn it. The same may be said of the Poignancy of Satyr; and the natural Images of ordinary Life in Comedy. It is one Thing to say, that an Heroic Poem virtually includes These; and another, that it actually puts them into Practice, or shews them at large in their proper Forms, and Dresses. I do not mention Tragedy; because That is so nearly ally'd to Heroic Poetry, that there is no Dispute or Question concerning it. An Epic Poem then is the same to all the other Kinds of Poetry, as the *Primum Mobile* is to the System of the Universe, according to the Scheme of the ancient Astronomy: That great Orb including all the heavenly Bodies in it's Circumference, and whirling them round with it's own Motion. And then the Soul of the Poet, or rather of Poetry, informing this mighty, and regular Machine, and diffusing Life and Spirit thro' the whole Frame, resembles that *Anima Mundi*, that Soul of the World, according to the *Platonic*, and *Pythagorean* Philosophy, thus admirably represented in the Sixth *Æneid*:

Principio cœlum, ac terras, camposque liquentes,
Lucentemque globum Lunæ, Titaniaque astra
Spiritus intus alit, totamque infusa per artus
Mens agitat molem, & magno se corpore miscet.

Here we have at once the Soul of Poetry, and the Soul of the World: The one *exerted*, while the other is *described*. Whether there be any such Thing as the Last or not, we certainly perceive the First; and however That be, Nothing, in reality, can give us a justly resembling Idea of the Fabrick of an Heroic Poem; but That, which alone is superiour to it, the Fabrick of the Universe.

I speak of an Heroic Poem, properly so called; for I know of but Three, or Four, which deserve the Glory of That Title. And it's transcendent Excellence is doubtless the Reason, why so few have attempted a Work of this Nature; and fewer have succeeded in such their Attempts. *Homer* arose like Light at the Creation; and shone upon the World, which (at least so far as we know) was, with respect to that kind of Light, in total Darkness, before his Appearing. Such was the Fire, and Vivacity of his Spirit; the Vastness, and Fecundity of his Invention; the Majesty, and Sublimity of his Thoughts, and Expressions; that, notwithstanding his Errours and Defects, which must be acknowledged, his controuling, and over-bearing Genius demanded those prodigious Honours, which in all Ages have been justly paid him. I say, notwithstanding his Errours and Defects: for it would have been strange indeed, had he been chargeable with None; or had he left no room to be refined, and improved upon by any Successour.

This was abundantly performed by *Virgil*; whose *Æneis* is therefore only not perfect, because it did not receive his last Hand. Tho', even as it now is, it comes the nearest to Perfection of any Heroic Poem; and indeed of any Poem whatsoever, except another of his Own: I mean his *Georgicks*; which I look upon to be the most Consummate of all human Compositions: It's Author for Genius and Judgment, for Nature and Art, joined together, and taken one with another, being the greatest, and best of all human Writers. How little Truth soever there may be in the Prodigies which are said to have attended his Birth; certain it is, that a Prodigy was then born; for He himself was such: And when God made That Man, He seems to have design'd to shew the World how far the Powers of mere human Nature can go, and how much they are capable of performing. The Bent of his Mind was turned to Thought, and Learning in general; and to Poetry, and Philosophy in particular. Which we are assured of not only from the Spirit and Genius of his Works; but from the express Account which he gives of himself, in Those sweet Lines of the second *Georgick*:

Me vero primum dulces ante omnia Musæ
(Quarum sacra fero, ingenti perculsus amore)
Accipiant, cœlique vias, & sydera monstrent.
Defectus solis varios, lunæque labores;
Unde tremor Terris, quâ vi maria alta tumescant
Objicibus ruptis, rursusque in seipsa residant.
Quid tantum oceano properent se tingere soles
Hyberni, vel quæ tardis mora noctibus obstet.

It is true, he here only tells us of his Inclination to Natural Philosophy; but then he tells it us in Poetry: As few Things are more nearly related.

For his Temper, and Constitution; if We will believe Mr. *Dryden*,[5] it was Phlegmatick, and Melancholick: As *Homer*'s was Sanguine, and Cholerick, and This, he says, is the Reason of the different Spirit, which appears in the Writings of those two great Authors. I make no doubt, but that *Virgil*, in his *natural Disposition, as a Man*, was rather Melancholick; as, I believe, most learned, and contemplative Men ever were, and ever will be. And therefore how does he breath the very Soul of a Poet, and of a Philosopher; when in the Verses immediately following Those above-cited, he thus expresses the Thoughtfulness of both those Tempers, as well as the peculiar Modesty of his Own!

Sin has nè possim naturæ accedere partes
Frigidus obstiterit circum præcordia sanguis;
Rura mihi, & rigui placeant in vallibus amnes,
Flumina amem, silvasque inglorius.——

Methinks, I *see* him, while I read Those Verses; I am sure I *feel* him. How delightful must it be, to enjoy so sweet a Retirement! What a Glory, to be so inglorious! This, I say, is generally the Natural Make of learned, and ingenious Men; and *Homer* himself, notwithstanding his Poetical Fire, was in all probability of the same Complexion. But if we consider *Virgil as a Poet*; I hope to make it appear, before I have finished This Preface, that, *as such*, he wanted neither the Sanguine, nor the Cholerick; tho' at the same time I acknowledge a Man's *natural Temper* will *very much incline* him to one way of Thinking, and Writing, more than to another.

But tho' his *Genius* was thus perfect; yet I take his *most distinguishing* Character to be the incomparable *Accuracy* of his *Judgment*; and particularly his elegant, and exquisite *Brevity*. He is never luxuriant, never says any thing in vain: *We admire Others* (says Monsieur *Rapin*) *for what they say; but we admire* Virgil, *for what he does not say*. And indeed his very Silence is expressive, and even his Omissions are Beauties. Yet is his Brevity neither *dry*, nor *obscure*; so far otherwise, that he is both the *fullest*, and the *clearest* Writer in the World. He always, says enough, but never too much: And This is to be observed in him, as well when he insists upon a Thing, as when he slightly passes it over, when his Stile is long, and flowing, as when it is short, and concise; in This Sense, he is brief, even where he enlarges; and while he rolls like a Torrent, he has nothing frothy, or redundant. So that to Him, of all Mankind, are Those famous Verses of Sir *John Denham* most particularly applicable:

Tho' deep, yet clear; tho' gentle, yet not dull;
Strong, without Rage; without O'erflowing, full.

Meaning *Rage* properly so called; not the *Poetical Fury*. For That He was very far from wanting; as will be seen in it's proper Place. His avoiding Redundancy therefore proceeded neither from Poverty, nor Parsimony; but from Elegancy, and Exactness. So correct is he in Those Parts of his Writings which are allowed to be finished; that I have often thought what a Treasure That Man would be possessed of (were such a Thing possible) who could procure the Filings of his Poems; and shew the World what *Virgil* would *not* shew it. The very Chippings of Those Diamonds would be more valuable than the richest Jewel of the *Indies*.

I have already said enough to involve my self in the now unavoidable Comparison between *Homer*, and *Virgil*; which has so much employ'd the Speculations of the Learned. Because it will be justly expected that I should endeavour at least to give some Reasons for my Assertions; or rather for my *Opinion*: For I desire that my *Assertions* may all along be understood to imply no more. As to *Homer*, nothing can be farther from my Thoughts than to defraud that prodigious Man of his due Praise. I have before said a little of it; and (would the Limits of this Discourse permit) could with Pleasure enlarge upon that Subject. Many of his Faults, as they are called, are indeed no Faults; but only charged upon him by ignorant Pretenders to Criticism: Others, if they are really so, are not His, but are entirely to be imputed to the Manners and Customs of the Age in which he writ: And even those which are least justifiable are to be excused upon this single Consideration, that he was the first of his Species. No Science starts into Perfection at it's Birth: And it is amazing that the Works of this great Poet come so near it as they do. Thus as to himself: Then as to others; his Glory in Point of Precedency is uncontestable; he is the Father of Poets, and of Poetry; and *Virgil* particularly has copy'd from him in a multitude of Instances. But after all, the Question is; Whether upon the whole, *Homer*'s or *Virgil's be the best Poems*, as we have them now; setting aside all *external Considerations*, relating to Times, and Customs; Inventing, and Borrowing; Precedency, and Succession; Master, and Scholar; and regarding only the *internal Advantages*, and *Disadvantages*, Beauties, and Faults of both; upon the Foundations of Nature, and Art, of Truth, and Reason. *Homer*'s Faults are to be excused: I am very glad of it; for I have an exceeding Honour, and

Love for him. But still *They are Faults*. Has *Virgil* so many? I mean too in Proportion, and allowing for the unequal Length of their Writings. *Virgil* imitated *Homer*, and borrowed from him: But did he not *improve*, as well as *imitate*; and by borrowing, and adding to his own vast Fund what the other never parted with, grow richer than him from whom he so borrowed? In a word, did he not out of two very good Poems make a better than either of them, or than both of them put together? I am sensible it may be said on the other hand, that *Homer* had the *Disadvantage*, as well as *Glory* of being the First: He had no body to rely upon, but himself; whereas *Virgil* had *Homer*'s Materials, besides his own. All this I acknowledge; nay at present, and for Argument's sake, let *Homer*'s be the *greater Glory*: Still is not *Virgil*'s the *best Poem*? For I agree that in these Comparisons we ought to make a Distinction between the *Man*, and the *Work*. Or if we must make the Comparison in the former respect; *Homer* was *Virgil*'s Master, Father, what you please: But nothing is more common, than for the Scholar to excel the Master, and the Son the Father. I think we ought to lay aside the Prejudices of an undue Veneration for the *greatest Antiquity*, and argue only from *Reason*; and that not only in the Comparison of the Ancients with one another; but even in That of the Ancients with the Moderns. I have a very great Honour for the *Greeks* and *Romans*; but 'tis because their Writings are generally *good*, not because they are *ancient*: And when we think they are otherwise than good, I cannot imagine why we should not say so; provided it be with Modesty, and with a due Deference to the Opinions of Those who differ from us, whether they be dead or living. The famous Dispute about Ancient and Modern Learning would, I believe, be soon determined; were it not for unreasonable Prejudices to each of Those Names respectively. The Ancients, *as such*, have the Advantage in This, that they ought to be honoured as the Inventers of most Arts and Sciences; but then the Moderns, *as such*, have the Advantage in This, that besides their own Strength and Sagacity, they have the Models of the Ancients to improve upon: And very strange it would be, if they should not improve in some things, as well as lose in others.

I shall give the particular Reasons for my Opinion of these two great Poets, before I finish: In the mean time, I hope the Reader will excuse my Rambling. I am very sensible that I shall not only differ in judgment from many Criticks of great Name, both Ancient and Modern; but that I am like to fall under the ready, and natural Censure of being prejudiced my self, while I warn against it in others. All I can say, is, that I have endeavoured to divest my self of it as much as possible; but cannot be positive that I am entirely free from it; being well aware that nothing in the World is more difficult. For I am sure I have followed *One* Precept of my Lord *Roscommon*, in his excellent Essay on Translated Verse:

Examine how your Humour is inclin'd,
And which the ruling Passion of your Mind;
Then seek a Poet who that way does bend,
And chuse an Author, as you chuse a Friend.

And as this is *One* Circumstance, which is like to make a Man succeed, as a *Translator*, so it is like to make him err, as a *Judge*. For this Sort of Friendship (like all others) will certainly incline us to be partial in favour of the Person whom we praise, or defend. It is in This, as in every thing else; the Affections will be apt to biass the Understanding; and doubtless a Man in a great measure judges This, or That way of Writing to be best, because it is most agreeable to his own natural Temper. Thus, for Example; One Man judges (as he calls it) *Horace*'s Satyrs to be the best; Another is for *Juvenal*'s: When, all this while, strictly speaking, they may not so much differ in *Judgment*, as *Inclination*: For each of them perhaps will allow Both to be best *in their Kind*; but the one is chiefly *delighted* with this Kind, and the other with that; and *there* is all the real Difference between them. And tho' this does not exactly parallel the present Case; the Poems of *Homer* and *Virgil* being more of the same Species, than the Satyrs of *Horace* and *Juvenal*; yet it comes very near it: and the Word *Species* will admit of more Distinction than is commonly imagined: These two Heroic Poets being very different in their *Turn*, and *Manner* of Thinking, and Writing. But after all, there are in Nature and Reason certain Rules by which we are to judge in these Matters, as well as in others; and there are still such things as Truth and Falshood, notwithstanding Partiality and Prepossession. And this I can assure my Reader, I am not prejudiced in Behalf of my Author, by attempting to be his Translator; for I was of the same Opinion, before I had the least Thought of this daring Enterprize. However, I do not pretend to decide as a Judge, but only to argue as an Advocate; and a Man may be allowed to plead with Prejudice, tho' he always ought to determine without it: For it may do no Mischief at the Bar, tho it be intolerable upon the Bench. But that my Reader may not be misguided by it, upon a Supposition that I am; I desire him to consider, that as I differ from some great Criticks, so I have the Authority of others to support my Opinion. I need not insist upon *Scaliger*, *Rapin*, and the incomparable Earl of *Roscommon*, whose Judgments upon this Point are very well known; but I will produce the Words of *Macrobius*, as collected by *la Cerda*,[6] because he is commonly supposed to be in the other Interest. It is true, in the Comparison of particular Passages, he generally prefers *Homer*; yet he says, *Virgilius Homero ditior, locupletior, cultior, purior, clarior, fortior vi argumentorum, diligentior, observantior, uberior, pulchrior.* "*Virgil* is richer, and fuller than *Homer*, neater, purer, clearer, stronger in the Force of his Arguments, more diligent, more observing, more copious, more beautiful." Thus, I say, he speaks, as he is represented by the above-mentioned Commentator; who only pretends to have picked up those Words from several scattered Passages in his Writings: Whether they are faithfully collected, or no (for he does not quote the particular Places) I have not had the Patience to examine, nor am I at all solicitous to know. It would be endless to cite *Scaliger* upon this Subject; and besides, when I agree with him, it is rather in his Praise of *Virgil*, than in his Dispraise of *Homer*. I am far from being of his Opinion in some Particulars, and farther from approving of his Way and Manner of Proceeding. He inveighs against *Homer* with as much Bitterness, as if he had a personal Quarrel with him; prosecutes him with all the Malice of Criticism, and that too sometimes false Criticism; and is upon the whole highly injurious to the Character of that wonderful Poet. Yet I cannot on the other side agree with Madam *Dacier*, who is at least even with *Scaliger*, by calling him the worst Critick in the World: *Le plus mechant Critique du Monde*, are the very Words she uses. On the contrary, I think, he is generally upon these Occasions rather Hyperbolical in his Expressions, than Erroneous in his Judgment. I am indeed amazed at the Confidence of Monsieur *de la Motte*, who treats *Homer* with the greatest Freedom, and almost with Contempt, when at the same time he acknowledges he does not understand one Word of his Language. For my self, I have nothing to say, but that I have a Right to deliver my Sentiments, as well as another; and, to use the Words of that noble Poet and Critick above-mentioned,

I speak my private, but impartial Sense,
With Freedom, and I hope without Offence.

And here I cannot but observe, that tho' I am charmed with that fine Turn of his, after having remarked upon some supposed Faults in *Homer*;

But I offend; Virgil *begins to frown,*
And Horace *looks with Indignation down;*
My blushing Muse with conscious Fear retires,
And whom they like implicitly admires:

Tho', I say, I am charmed with the Elegancy of the Poet, the Modesty of the Critick, and the courtly Politeness of the Nobleman; and tho', as I shall observe hereafter, I am not of his Opinion, as to the Particulars he takes notice of, in the Verses preceding: yet I do not understand why, for disapproving of some things in *Homer*, he should apprehend either the Frowns of *Virgil*, or the Indignation of *Horace*. As *Virgil* saw the Beauties of *Homer*, while he imitated them; he no less saw his Errours, while he avoided them. And as to *Horace*, that *Nil molitur inepte*, in one Place, and—— *Quandoque bonus dormitat Homerus*, in another, must be regarded as Hyperboles; the one as an Auxesis, the other as a Meiôsis. Not but that upon the whole, he certainly admired *Homer*; nor would he have been the good Judge he was, if he had not. But as he was acquainted with the *Iliad*, and the *Odyssee*, so had he lived to have been as well acquainted with the *Æneis*; would he not have preferred the last, before both the first? Those who differ from me will say he *would not*; and 'tis altogether as easy for me to say he *would*. The same, and more, may be remarked of *Aristotle*; who was perfectly acquainted with *Homer*, but not at all with *Virgil*.

Invention, Fire, and Judgment, will, I think, include all the Requisites of an Epic Poem. The Action, the Fable, the Manners, the Compass, and Variety of Matter, seem to be properly comprehended under the First of these; yet not so as to exclude the Two last. For the particular Disposition of them all is an Act of the Judgment, as the first Creating of them is an Act of Invention; and Fire, tho' distinct from Invention, and Judgment, has a near Relation to them Both, as it assists the one, and is to be regulated by the other.

By those who commonly discourse of Heroic, and Dramatic Poetry, the Action, and the Fable seem not to be sufficiently distinguished. The Action is a great Achievement of some illustrious Person, attended with an important and memorable Event. The Fable is that Complication of Incidents, Episodes, and other Circumstances, which tend to the carrying on of the Action, or give Reasons for it, or at least embellish and adorn it. I make this Distinction; because Episodes are such, as are either absolutely necessary, or very requisite. Of the former sort is that long Narration of *Æneas*, I mean in the main Substance of it, which is the entire Subject of the Second, and Third Books. This perhaps will not by some be allowed to be an Episode; because, I think, it is not commonly called so: For that Word is generally appropriated to *Actions*, and therefore will be supposed not applicable to a *Narration*. But I think we shall speak more clearly; if by that Word we mean (as indeed the [7]Etymology of it imports) whatsoever is *adventitious* to the grand Action of the Poem, connected to it, or inserted in it; whether it be it self an Action, or no. And there is Ground enough to distinguish This from the immediate, and direct Train, or Course of the main Action it self; and to shew what may, and may not, be called an Episode. For Example; The Sailing of the *Trojan* Fleet from *Sicily* in the First Book, it's Arrival there again at the Beginning of the Fifth, and it's Sailing from thence at the End of that Book; The Landing at *Cumæ* in the Beginning of the Sixth; and in another Part of *Italy*, at the Beginning of the Seventh; The whole Operations of that Book, and so of all the rest, wherever the Heroe himself, or his Armies for him, either with or without his Presence, are directly engaged in the great Affair to be carry'd on, are, all of them, so many successive Parts of one, and the same Action (the great Action of the Poem) continued in a direct Line, and flowing in it's proper Channel. But where any Part comes under any one of the Bye-Characters above-mentioned, it is properly an Episode, whether it be an Action, or a

Narration. The long Recital of Adventures in the Second and Third Books is not an *Action*, but it is *Necessary*: The Expedition of *Nisus* and *Euryalus* in the Ninth is not *Necessary*, but it is an *Action*: And Both are Episodes. Which brings us back to the Distinction before taken notice of, between Incidents and Episodes, and the several Kinds of the latter. All Episodes are Incidents; but it is not so on the Reverse. The Storm in the First Book, driving the Fleet on the Coast of *Carthage*, is an Incident, but not an Episode; because the Heroe himself, and the whole Body of his Forces, are concerned in it; and so it is a *direct*, not a *collateral* Part of the main Action. But even Episodes (as I said) must carry on the main Action, or give Reasons for it, or at least embellish it: And therefore I said they are either *absolutely necessary*, or *very requisite*. The Narration in the Second and Third Books is not a *Part* of the Action; but it *gives Reasons* for it, and so is *Necessary*: The Adventures of *Nisus* and *Euryalus* in the Ninth Book, of *Mezentius* in the Tenth, and of *Camilla* in the Eleventh, are all *requisite*, but not *absolutely necessary*; and yet they are properly *Parts* of the main Action, tho' *collateral*, not *direct*. The Loves of *Dido* and *Æneas* in the Fourth Book, the Sports at the Tomb of *Anchises* in the Fifth, the Description of Hell in the Sixth, the Story of *Cacus*, and the Decorations of the Shield in the Eighth, are all supposed by some to be entirely ornamental, and no Parts of the main Action. And This perhaps they may imagine to be a great Point yielded to the Disadvantage of *Virgil*. Admitting it were so, *Homer* would gain nothing by it; most of them being taken from him, and he having more of such *Excrescencies*, if they must be so called. But This in Reality is no reasonable Objection against either. The Episode of *Dido* and *Æneas* shall be considered in my Remarks upon the Fourth Book. The Descent into Hell is a direct Part of the Action; the Heroe going thither to consult his Father's Ghost concerning the Operations of the War, and the future Fate of Himself, and his Posterity (for *all* Action, even in an Heroic Poem, does not consist in *Fighting*:) And it would be very strange, if, in a Work of such a Length, the Poet might not be allowed to take that Occasion, to describe the Regions thro' which his Heroe passed, and to make the noblest, and most surprizing Description that ever the World saw. The same may be said of the Casting, and Engraving of the Shield, which contains a considerable Part of the *Roman* History; as does the Speech of *Anchises* in the foregoing Division; both introduced with exquisite Art, and Judgment. For the rest; granting that they are purely ornamental; and that while the Poet is describing them, the Action stands still, as the Criticks express themselves: There let it stand, with all my heart, 'till *Virgil* thinks fit to set it a going again. If the Action stands still, I am sure the Poem does not; and the Reader, I think, must be very phlegmatick, if his Spirits do. What if those Episodes are not Parts of the Action? They are Parts of the Poem, and with the greatest Skill inferred in it. What if they are not absolutely *necessary*? They are very *convenient*; and that is sufficient. For if we allow that they are entirely ornamental, we deny that they are impertinent, or superfluous; no Things in the World being more uniform, or more naturally and elegantly connected. Nor does *Virgil* ever commit the Fault of those whom *Horace* justly condemns; by whom

Purpureus, late qui splendeat, unus & alter
Assuitur pannus——

But the Foundation of all this wrong Criticism, is the Errour of reducing an Heroic Poem to the narrow Rules of the *Stage*. For tho' the Drama be, in some Respects, more perfect than the Epopée, in others it is inferiour. And it is not *Virgil*'s Fault, if we will not distinguish between the Building of a House, and of a City; or between that of a City, and of the Universe. In a Work of such an Extent as an Epic Poem, and all delivered in Narration, not represented by Action, these Interruptions of the main Business (especially when they are some of the most beautiful Parts of the Poem, as they always are in *Virgil*'s) are so far from being Improprieties, that they are Excellencies. This Variety is a Relief to the Mind of the Reader; who is more diverted by the alternate Rest, and Rapidity of the Action, than he would be by it's perpetual Motion. Nay the Mind is therefore the more in perpetual Motion, (tho' in several kinds of it) than if the Action really were so. For the Poem, as I observed, does not stand still, tho' the Action may.

If what I have discoursed upon Episodes be not in the usual, I think it is in the clearer way of Expressing; and as such I propose it to others. *Bossu*, in his excellent Treatise of Epic Poetry, has some nice Distinctions concerning them; which to me are more subtile, than perspicuous: But that, I am sensible, may be my Fault, not his. And yet he seems not to distinguish enough, when he says all Episodes are necessary Parts of the Action, and makes no Difference between Necessary, and Convenient. Nay he appears to be inconsistent[8] with himself upon this Head, and to mistake the Sense of *Aristotle*. To the Doctrine of which Philosopher I think my Account is more agreeable. For after he has represented the Action of the *Odyssée* in a direct Line, as I have That of the *Æneis*; he immediately adds,[9] *This then is proper; the rest are Episodes.* By the Word *Proper*, I understand Immediately, and Directly Necessary. But he no where says that all Episodes are so in any Sense; but leaves that Matter at large. For tho' his *French* Translators, *Bossu*, and *Dacier* (which latter, I think, is in the same Errour with the former) use the same Word *Proper*, when apply'd to Episodes, as when apply'd to the main Action; yet the Words[10] in the Original are different. *Bossu* argues, that the litteral Signification of the Word *Episode*, [something *adventitious*] cannot take place; because an Episode must not be *added*, or *superinduced*, but naturally *flow*, or *arise* from the Subject. As if a new Person could not enter a Room to a Company already there assembled, without being impertinent: Surely his Coming may not only be proper, but necessary; tho' I confess it may not be necessary, and yet be proper: Which is the very thing I would say of Episodes. According to this, when *Virgil* says in the Seventh Book,

Hos super advenit *Volsca de gente Camilla*;

That Heroine is a mere Intruder; and her Story afterwards in the Eleventh Book is no *Episode*. In short, it matters not whether we say those Incidents *flow*, or *arise from* the Subject; or are *added*, and *connected to it*; or *inserted*, and *interwoven with* it: If they are *natural*, and *proper Parts* of the *Poem*, That is sufficient; all the rest is a Dispute about Words, and of no Importance, or Significancy. However it be, I think I cannot better represent the several sorts of Episodes which I have mentioned, than by an Instance nearly ally'd to my Subject; I mean that of a General making a Campaign. All the important Undertakings, and Performances of Himself, or the Gross of his Army, or Both, in pursuance of the Design proposed, are direct Parts of the main Action; and so far the Campaign, and the Poem agree even in Terms. If he sitting in his Tent either gives, or hears, the Recital of something past, the Knowledge of which is absolutely necessary to the Prosecution of his Enterprize; This indeed is not Action: But still it was said to be absolutely necessary in order to the Prosecution of his Enterprize. And so is that Narration of *Æneas* in the Second, and Third Books, in order to the carrying on of the Action, and to shew the Reason of it. This in War would not be called an Episode; but it is so in Poetry. Should the same General detach a Part of his Army upon a particular Expedition; and the Commander of that Body behave himself with uncommon Gallantry, and attempt something very extraordinary, and to be distinguished in History; whether he succeeded in that Attempt or not: This would indeed be a Part of the Campaign; but perhaps not a necessary one; because the Campaign might have subsisted, and have been successful, or unsuccessful, with it, or without it. Such are the Episodes of *Nisus* and *Euryalus*; of *Mezentius*; and of *Camilla*. The Case of the same General's being for some time diverted from Action by an Amour, or some such Incident, shall be considered in my Remarks upon the Fourth Book. But should he in Time of Inaction, tho' the Campaign still continued, entertain his Officers and Soldiers with warlike Sports and Recreations; or hear the Relation of some memorable Adventure, in the Place where he encamped (like the Adventure of *Hercules*, and *Cacus*) tho' no way concerning his own Affairs: These indeed would not be Parts of the Action of his Campaign; but still might be very properly recorded in History, and afford great Delight to the Reader; who would by no Means be offended either with the General, or the Historian; nor think the History of that Campaign to be less of a Piece, because the warlike Operations were for some Time suspended. For we must still remember, that tho' an Epic Poem be widely different from History in many Circumstances; yet it is more nearly ally'd to it, than any Dramatic Piece whatsoever. The learned Reader, I fear, will think I might have troubled him with fewer Words upon this Subject, but such Readers I presume not to instruct: What I have said may not perhaps be altogether unuseful to Those who are less conversant in these Matters: To acquaint them with which, nothing can contribute more, than clear Ideas annexed to the Words, *Action, Fable, Incident,* and *Episode*: All which (especially the last) are ill understood by many, who yet use them with the greatest Freedom and Familiarity.

Now if my Opinion be not received, I hope my avowed Ignorance will at least be excused; while I confess, that tho' I very clearly apprehend the Settling of the *Trojan* Colony in *Italy* to be the Action of the *Æneis*; and the Return of *Ulysses* to be the Action of the *Odyssée*: yet I do not so well understand how the Anger of *Achilles* comes to be called the Action of the *Iliad*. For besides that Anger is a Passion, not an Action: And if you mean the immediate Effect of that Anger, not the Anger it self; Standing still, and doing nothing (which was the Consequence of that Heroe's Resentment) can as little be called an Action as the Other; I say, not to insist upon This, tho' it is by no means so trivial a Nicety as some may suppose; the Anger of *Achilles* is not the *main Subject* of the Poem, nor the chief Hinge upon which it turns. The Action of it seems to be the Conquest of *Troy*; the Fable, the *Trojan* War; and the Anger of *Achilles*, an important Incident, serving to aggrandize the Heroe, and consequently the Action, and to render them more illustrious; as also at the same time to convey that useful Moral, concerning the fatal Effects of Discord and Contention. It will be said, that what I have mentioned is not the Action of the Poem, because *Homer* has not proposed it as such: But may it not be as well replied, that *it is* the Action of the Poem; and therefore he *should have* proposed it as such? For what is the Action, appears from the Stress and Turn of the Work, not from the Title or Exordium; from the End, not from the Beginning: And of This the Readers are to judge, as well as of any thing else. Did not *Homer* then know the Action of his own Poem? Yes questionless; but he did not mention it in his Proposition; which may possibly be chargeable upon him as an Errour: He mentions the most important Incident, but omits the Action. Had the Exordium set forth the Defeat of the *Trojans*, and the Destruction of *Troy*, with such a Clause as this, "Tho' that great Event was suspended by the fatal Anger of *Achilles*, Ἡ μυρί' Ἀχαιοῖς ἄλγε' ἔθηκε, and so on, as it now stands; it would, in my humble Opinion, have been more unexceptionable than it is at present. But I beg Pardon for even seeming to pretend to correct *Homer*; and speak This with all possible Submission. It is true, the Conquest of *Troy* is not compleated in the *Iliad*; no more is the Settlement of the *Trojans* by the Building of the Heroe's City in the *Æneis*:

But *Hector* is killed in the one; as *Turnus* is in the other; and the Consequences of Both are very visible. I acknowledge indeed, that those of the former are not so near in view as those of the latter. But tho' *Virgil* in his *Æneis*, and *Homer* himself in his *Odyssée*, inform us that the Death of *Hector* was not the immediate Cause of the Destruction of *Troy*; the War continuing with great Obstinacy for a considerable time after that Heroe's Death; as the Stratagem of the Wooden Horse was the immediate Cause of that City's Destruction; And tho' *Homer* confines the direct Action of his *Iliad* only to a Part of the *Trojan* War: Yet he takes in the Whole from the Amour of *Paris* and *Helen* to the Burning of the Town, by way of Narration, and by way of Prophecy; which Artifice, next to Fiction, is the most proper Character of Epick Poetry, as distinguished from History. For the Invention of This, we are (at least so far as we know) solely obliged to *Homer*. And for This alone, if he had done nothing else, he would have merited that immortal Glory, which for This, and for a thousand other Excellencies, he now most justly possesses.

The Shortness of the Time, and the Simplicity of the Action, are Circumstances which, in the Opinion of some, give the *Iliad* a great Advantage over the *Æneis*. The first mentioned would be no such Advantage; if what *Ruæus* says were true; that the *Iliad* takes up a Year: For Monsieur *Segrais* has made it plain to a Demonstration, that the *Æneis* takes up no more. But I wonder *Ruæus* should affirm That of the *Iliad*; when it is manifest that the whole Action includes no more than forty seven Days. As to the Simplicity, or Singleness of which; if That be the Action which I apprehend, (for, out of Deference to the commonly received Opinion, I do not insist upon it) the Action is more complex, than it is generally supposed. But admitting that in the *Iliad* the Action is more simple, as well as the Time shorter, than in the *Æneis*: Doubtless a single Action is better than a complicated one, *as such*; or in other Words, it is better, if it can be made equally entertaining. But there is the Difficulty: And for that Reason, it is a Question not yet decided, whether, even in Pieces for the Theatre, complicated Actions, all things considered, be not, generally speaking, preferable to single ones. And there is yet more Reason to prefer the former in an Epic Poem; which is of a far wider Extent, and partakes the Nature of History in some Respects, as well as of the Drama in others. "*Virgil* (says Mr. *Pope*[11]) for want of so warm a Genius [as *Homer*'s] aided himself by taking in a more extensive Subject, as well as a greater Length of Time; and contracted the Design of both *Homer*'s Poems into one, which is yet but a fourth Part as large as his." The supposed Coolness of *Virgil*'s Genius shall be considered hereafter. At present I acknowledge he took what he thought proper out of the *Iliad* and *Odyssée*, tho' he did not take his *Design* from either; and his first six Books resemble the *Odyssée*, as the last six do the *Iliad*: And his one Poem, 'tis granted, is in Number of Books no more than a Quarter of *Homer*'s two. But in This the Advantage seems to be on his Side. For there is, if I do not greatly miscalculate, as much important Matter, and as great a Variety of Incidents, in *Virgil*'s Twelve, as in *Homer*'s Forty eight. And yet is *Virgil*'s Poem too much crouded, and the Matter too thick? I think not. Are not *Homer*'s, on the contrary, too lean? and is not the Matter too thinly spred? I think it is. When I say a greater Number of Incidents; I do not mean more Men killed, more Battles fought, more Speeches spoke, and the like: Those are not Incidents; and I own *Homer* has many more of them than *Virgil*. Mr. *Pope* admires the Variety of *Homer*'s Battles for this Reason, that tho' they are so numerous they are not tedious. This is *extraordinary* indeed, if it be *true*. But whether a Thing be tedious or not, is Matter of Experience, rather than of Judgment; and so every particular Person must speak as he finds. Upon his Multitude of Speeches, the most ingenious Gentleman above-mentioned, (who was certainly *born a Poet*, if ever Man was) has this Remark: "It is hardly credible, in a Work of such a Length, how small a Number of Lines are employed in Narration. In *Virgil* the Dramatic Part is less in proportion to the Narrative." It is so; and even in proportion to the different Length of their Works, *Homer* has undoubtedly more Speeches than *Virgil*; too many, in my humble Opinion. *Homer* has not enough of the Narrative Part; but *Virgil* has enough of the Dramatic; if it must be so called. For, by the way, (tho' I very well remember that *Aristotle* applies this Word to the Epopée, and have elsewhere taken notice of it, and have observed from Monsieur *Dacier*, that he uses it in a different Sense from This of which we are now speaking) I do not understand why Speech-making in an Heroic Poem must be called *Dramatic*; and by virtue of that Name pass for a Beauty. The Drama indeed consists wholly of Speeches; but then they are spoken by the Persons themselves, who are actually introduced and represented; not related and recited by the Author as spoken by others, as they always are in an Epic Poem. *Those* are both agreeable, and necessary; *These*, if they take up far the greatest Part of the Work, being inserted by the everlasting Repetition of those introducing, and closing interlocutory Tags, Καὶ μιν φωνήσας, Τὸν δ' αὖτε προσέειπε, Ὣς ἔφατ', Τὸν δ' ἀπαμειβόμενος, &c. are apt to tire the Reader; nor does the Word *Dramatic* at all lessen the Disgust which they give him. I am aware too, that setting aside the Word *Dramatic*, *Aristotle* expresly declares for a Multitude of Speeches, and little Narration in Epic Poetry: But then I beg Leave once for all to make a Remark upon this Subject, which may be applied to some others; That *Aristotle*'s Precepts are formed upon *Homer*'s Practice; no *other* Heroic Poet having *then* appeared in the World. But since the Case is now quite altered, to give *Homer* the Preference to *Virgil* upon Rules entirely drawn from his own Practice, would be *begging the Question* even in the Judgment of *Aristotle* as a Logician, whatever might be his Opinion as a Critick. Not but that, after all, a far greater Part even of *Virgil*'s Poem is employed in Speeches, than one would imagine without a *very close Attention*. If I may judge of others by my self, we are deceived by him in this Particular, (so exquisite is his Art) and even after frequent Readings do not ordinarily take notice that there are so many Speeches in his *Æneis* as there really are: An infallible Sign that they are excellent in themselves, and most skilfully introduced and connected. I agree that in an Epic Poem they ought to be *very numerous*; tho' I do not ground that Opinion upon the Reason which *Aristotle* assigns; *viz*. That otherwise a Poet would not be an *Imitator*. For is there no *Imitation* but in *Speeches*? What are *Descriptions*?

By more Incidents then I do not mean (as I said) more Men killed, more Battles fought, more Speeches spoke; but more memorable and surprizing Events. Take these Poems therefore purely as Romances; and consider them only with regard to the History, and Facts contained in them, the Plots, the Actions, Turns, and Events; That of *Virgil* is more copious, full, various, and surprizing, and every way more entertaining, than Those of *Homer*. Then is there any Comparison between the Subjects of the Poems? Between the Anger of *Achilles*, (if That be the Subject of the *Iliad*) and the Return of *Ulysses* in Those of the Greek Poet; and the Founding of *Rome*, and the Glory of the *Romans* in That of the Latin one?

It is said by Mr. *Dryden*[12], and others, that *Homer*'s Moral is more Noble than *Virgil*'s; but for what Reason I know not. The Quarrel of *Achilles* and *Agamemnon* teaches us the ill Consequences of Discord in a State; and the Story of the Dogs, the Sheep, and the Wolf, in *Æsop*'s Fables, does the same.[13] This indeed is a very good Lesson; but it seems too narrow, and particular, to be the *Grand Moral* of an Heroic Poem. It is proper, if you please, to be *inserted* in such a Work; and many more as important as This are interspersed up and down, and mentioned among other Things, both in That of *Virgil*, and in Those of *Homer*. But how much more noble, extensive, and truly Heroic a Moral is This; That Piety to God, and Justice and Goodness to Men, together with true Valour, both Active, and Passive, (not such as consists in Strength, Intrepidity, and Fierceness only, which is the Courage of a *Tyger*, not of a Man) will engage Heaven on our Sides, and make both Prince, and People, victorious, flourishing, and happy? And This is the Moral of the *Æneis*, properly so called. For tho' *Virgil* had plainly another End in view, which was to conciliate the Affections of the *Roman* People to the new Government of *Augustus Cæsar*; upon which *Bossu*, and after him Mr. *Dryden*, have largely, and excellently discoursed: Yet this is rather of a Political, than of a Moral Nature. Mr. *Pope* seeming to acknowledge that the Moral of the *Æneis* is preferable to That of the *Iliad*, only says that the same Arguments upon which that Preference is grounded might set the *Odyssée* above the *Æneis*. But as he does not give Reasons for that Assertion, it will be sufficient to say, that there seems to me to be at least as much Morality in *Virgil*'s Poem, as in the *Odyssée* it self; and that particularly in the Characters of the Heroes, *Æneas* as much excels *Ulysses* in Piety, as *Achilles* does *Æneas* in rapid Valour. And for Virtue in general, the Point between the two Heroes last mentioned is entirely yielded by every Body in favour of *Virgil*'s; the very Moral of the *Iliad* requiring that it's Heroe should be immoral. But sure it is more artful and entertaining, as well as useful and instructive, to have the Moral of the Poem so cast and contrived, that the principal Person in it may be good and virtuous, as well as great and brave. It will be said, *Homer* could not avoid that Inconvenience; *Achilles* having a known Character before: It may be so; and I am glad of that Excuse: But still *so it is*; and it would have been *better*, if it had been *otherwise*. Or if you will have it as Mr. *Pope* puts it, (less, I think, to *Homer*'s Advantage) He did not design to do otherwise: "They blame him (says he) for not doing what he never designed: As because *Achilles* is not as good, and perfect a Prince as *Æneas*, when the very Moral of his Poem required a contrary Character." I wish then his Design had been *different*: Because if it had, it would have been *better*. If a Man does ill; is it an Answer to say, He designed to do so? The Account which *Horace* gives of *Achilles* is a very true one:

Impiger, iracundus, inexorabilis, acer,
Jura negat sibi nata, nihil non arrogat armis.

Heroic Virtues, no doubt! An admirable Character of a Demi-god!

But who will contend that the *Grecian* Poet is comparable to the *Roman*, in his exquisite Understanding of humane Nature, and particularly in his Art of moving the Passions? Which is one of the most distinguishing Characters of a Poet, and in which he peculiarly triumphs and glories. I mention only the fourth *Æneid*, (tho' an hundred other Instances might be mentioned) and desire That Book alone may be matched in this respect by all *Homer*'s Works put together. And yet I am not unmindful of several excellent pathetical Passages in both those immortal Poems.

What has been hitherto discoursed, includes both Judgment and Invention. That *Homer* excels *Virgil* in the latter of These, is generally taken for granted. That he invented *before* him, and invented *more*, is an undoubted Truth: But it does not from thence follow that he invented *better*, or that he had a *better Invention*. For to say that *Virgil* betrays a Barrenness of Genius, or Scantiness of Imagination, (even in comparison with *Homer*) is a most groundless, and unjust Reflection upon him. It is his exact Judgment which makes both his Fancy, and his Fire seem less to Some, than they really are. And then we must consider that it was the Fashion among the *Romans* to adopt all Learning of the *Greeks* into their own Language: It was so in

Oratory, and Philosophy, as well as in Poetry. And therefore it is no Consequence that *Virgil* was of a narrower Invention than *Homer* himself, because in many things he copied from him: And yet That Inference is continually made, and those things unreasonably confounded. And after all; *Virgil* did not copy so much from *Homer*, as some would make us believe; from whose Discourse, if we had no other Evidence, one would imagine the Latin to be little more than a Translation, and an Abridgment of the Greek. The admirable Choice of his Subject, and Heroe, for the Honour of his Country; his most artfully interweaving the *Roman* History, especially at those three remarkable Divisions in the First, the Sixth, and the Eighth Books; his Action, and the Main of his Fable; the exquisite Mechanism of his Poem, and the Disposition of it's Parts, are entirely his own; as are most of his Episodes: And I suppose it will be allowed that his Diction and Versification were not taken from *Homer*. To pass over many other things which might be mentioned, and some of which I shall mention in my Notes; Why must *Dido* and *Æneas* be copied from *Calypso* and *Ulysses*? The Reason is plain: *Dido* and *Calypso* were Women, (if the latter, being a Goddess, may be called so;) and *Ulysses* and *Æneas* were Men; and between those Men and Women there was a Love-Adventure, and a Heroe detained by it. That is all the Resemblance between the Persons immediately concerned. *Jupiter*'s Message by *Mercury* indeed is plainly taken from *Homer* by *Virgil*: But *Virgil* might very well think of that Imitation, after he had laid the Plan of *Dido*'s Episode; which is quite of another Nature from *Calypso*'s, and introduced with a quite different Design. For the same Reason, I suppose, the Conversation between *Venus* and *Jupiter* in the First *Æneid* must be taken from *Homer*; because *Thetis* has a Conference with that God (in favour of her Son too) in the First *Iliad*. *Virgil* mentions Sea and Land, Heaven and Earth, Horses and Chariots, Gods and Men; nay he makes use of Hexameter Verse, and the Letters of the Alphabet; and *Homer*, tho' in a different Language, had I confess, done all This before him. But where *Virgil* really does (as he often does) imitate *Homer*, how does he at the same time *exceed* him! What Comparison is there between the Funeral Games for *Patroclus*, and those for *Anchises*? Between the Descent of *Ulysses* into Hell, and that of *Æneas*? Between the merely ornamental Sculptures upon *Homer*'s *Vulcanian* Shield, and the *Roman* History, and the Triumphs of *Augustus* upon *Virgil*'s? In my Notes I shall be more particular: At present, I cannot forbear saying, that to be *such* an Improver is at least almost as much Glory, as to be the original Inventer.[14]

As the Case is stated between these two great Poets by the most moderate Criticks; *Homer* excelled in Fire, and Invention; and *Virgil* in Judgment. *Invention* has been already enough considered: *Judgment*, and *Fire* are farther to be discoursed of. That *Virgil* excelled in Judgment, we all allow. But *how far* did he excel? Did he not *very much*? Almost beyond Comparison? I shall here say very little of *Homer*'s Errours, and *Virgil*'s Excellencies in that Respect. The latter I shall speak of in my Notes; And the former I have no mind to: Both, because it has been so frequently, and largely done already; and also, because it is an uneasy Task; and I had much rather remark upon Beauties, than upon Faults; especially in one of the greatest Men that ever lived; and for whom I have an exceeding Love, and Veneration. I think he is unjustly censured by my Lord *Roscommon*, and Others, for his *Railing Heroes, and Wounded Gods*. The one was agreeable to the Manners of those Ages, which he best knew: And as to the other, Those who are thus wounded are subordinate Deities, and supposed to have Bodies, or certain Vehicles equivalent to them. Indeed, as *Jupiter* is invested with Omnipotence, and other Attributes of the supreme God; I know not how to account for his being bound and imprisoned by his Subjects, and requiring the Assistance of a Giant to release him: And tho' the *Wound* of *Mars* may be no Impropriety; yet his *Behaviour* upon it is very strange: He roars, and runs away, and tells his Father; and the God of War is the veriest Coward in the Field. Nor can I forbear thinking, notwithstanding all the Refinements of Criticks, and Commentators, that the Figure which *Vulcan* makes in the Synod of the Gods is a little improper, and unheroical. But, as I said, I care not to insist upon these Things; nor do I deny that *Virgil* has Faults, and that too in his first Six Books, which are most correct, and least liable to Exception. I shall in my Remarks take Notice of some Passages, which I think to be such. No *Mortal* was ever yet the Author of a Work absolutely perfect: There are but *Two* such in the World; if we may properly say so: For the *World* it self is one of them.

Virgil then greatly excelled *Homer* in Judgment: So much, that had he been greatly excelled by him in Fire, the Advantage, upon the Comparison in these two Respects, would have been on his Side. But I shall not consider, on the other hand, how far *Homer* exceeded *Virgil* in Fire; because I utterly deny that he exceeded him in it at all.

This, I am sensible, will seem a bold Assertion. Many who, upon the Whole, prefer *Virgil*, give him up here: Many, I say; for Some do not. And never was any Author more injured, than he has been, by some Criticks, especially *Modern ones*, in the Article of Genius, and Poetical Fire. What do these Gentlemen call Fire? Or how much Fire would they have? It is impossible to instance in Particulars here; I shall do That in my Notes: I can now only refer to some general Heads, among a Multitude more, which I cannot so much as mention. In the First Book, *Juno*'s Speech, *Æolus*, the Storm, the Beginning of *Dido*'s Passion: Almost the whole Second Book throughout: *Polyphemus*, and *Ætna* in the Third: The Sports, and the Burning of the Ships, in the Fifth: The Sibyl's Prophetick Enthusiasm, and the Descent into Hell in the Sixth: *Juno*'s Speech again, the Fury *Alecto*, the

Occasion of the War, and the Assembling of the Forces in the Seventh: The Story of *Cacus* in the Eighth, the *Cyclops*, and the Shield: In the Ninth, the Beginning of warlike Action; at

Hic subitam nigro glomerari pulvere nubem
Prospiciunt Teucri, & tenebras insurgere campis, &c.

Nisus and *Euryalus*; and the amazing Exploits of *Turnus* in the Enemy's City: In the Tenth, the Arrival of *Æneas* with his Fleet and Forces, at

Ardet apex capiti, cristisque à vertice flamma
Funditur, & vastos umbo vomit aureus ignes, &c.

It is needless, and would be almost endless, to recite the Rapidity of the War in the Tenth, Eleventh, and Twelfth Books; *Mezentius*, *Camilla*; the Speeches of *Turnus*, to *Drances*, to *Latinus*, to his Sister *Juturna*; and lastly, the single Combat between *Æneas* and Him:

At Pater Æneas, audito nomine Turni,
Deserit & muros, & summas deserit arces;
Præcipitatque moras omnes, opera omnia rumpit,
Lætitia exultans, horrendumque intonat armis:
Quantus Athos, &c.

Which reminds me, by the way, that the same Persons, who blame *Virgil* for want of Fire, blame his Heroe for want of Courage; and with just as much Reason. I agree, that each of these Poets in his Temper and Spirit extremely resembles his Heroe: And accordingly, *Homer* is no more superior to *Virgil* in *true Fire*, than *Achilles* is to *Æneas* in *true Courage*. But what necessarily supposes the Poetical Fire, and cannot subsist without it, has not been yet mentioned upon this Head; tho' it was taken Notice of upon another: I mean, *Moving the Passions*, especially those of Terrour and Pity. The Fourth Book throughout I have above referred to: The Death of *Priam*; The Meeting of *Æneas* and *Andromache*; *Nisus* and *Euryalus* again: *Evander*'s Concern for his Son before his Death, and his Lamentation after it; The Distress of *Juturna*, and the Fury in the Shape of an Owl flapping upon the Shield of *Turnus*, are some Instances selected out of many. The Truth is, (so far as it appears from their several Works) the *Greek* Poet knew little of the Passions, in comparison of the *Roman*.

It must be observed, that tho' most of the Instances, which I have now produced out of *Virgil*, are taken from warlike Adventures; yet it is a great Errour to think (as some do) that all Fire consists in Quarrelling and Fighting: as do nine Parts in ten of *Homer*'s, in his *Iliad*. The Fire we are speaking of, is *Spirit* and *Vivacity*; *Energy* of *Thought*, and *Expression*; which way soever it *affects us*; whether it fires us by *Anger*, or *otherwise*; nay, tho' it *does not fire us at all*, but even produces a *quite contrary Effect*. However it may sound like a Paradox; it is the Property of this Poetical Flame to chill us with Horrour, and make us weep with Pity, as well as to kindle us with Indignation, Love, or Glory: It is it's Property to cool, as well as to burn; and Frost and Snow are it's Fuel, as much as Sulphur.

——Jamque volans, apicem, & latera ardua cernit
Atlantis duri, cœlum qui vertice fulcit;
Atlantis, cinctum assidue cui nubibus atris
Piniferum caput, & vento pulsatur, & imbri:
Nix humeros infusa tegit, tum flumina mento
Præcipitant senis, & glacie riget horrida barba.

In these Lines we have the Images of a hoary old Man, a vast rocky Mountain, black Clouds, Wind and Rain, Ice and Snow; One shrinks, and shivers, while one reads them: And yet the World affords few better Instances of Poetical Fire; which is as much shewn in describing a Winter-piece, as in describing a Battle, or a Conflagration. However, as it appears from the Examples before cited, *Virgil* was not deficient even in That sort of Fire which is commonly called so, the fierce, the rapid, the fighting: And where he either shews not That, or none at all, 'tis not because he *can't*, but because he *w'on't*; because 'tis not proper. To explain my self, I refer the Reader to my Remark upon V. 712 of the First Book. Excepting some uncorrect Verses, *Virgil* never flags: Or when he appears to do so, it is on purpose; according to that most true Opinion of my Lord *Roscommon*:

For I mistake; or far the greatest Part
Of what some call Neglect, was study'd Art.
When Virgil *seems to trifle in a Line;*
'Tis like a Warning-piece, which gives the Sign,
To wake your Fancy, and prepare your Sight
To reach the noble Height of some unusual Flight.

His very Negligences are accurate, and even his Blemishes are Beauties. Besides; a considerable Number of Verses together may have little, or no Fire in them; and yet be very graceful, and deserve great Praise. *Virgil* (which I think is not so observable in *Homer*) can be elegant, and admirable, without being in a Hurry, or in a Passion. He is sometimes higher indeed, and sometimes lower: but he always flies; and that too (as Mr. *Segrais* judiciously observes) always at a Distance from the Ground: He rises, and sinks, as he pleases; but never flutters, or grovels. Can the same be as truly said of *Homer*? His Fire in the main is divine; but as I think he has too much of it in some Places, has he not too little in others? Mr. *Dryden* says, [15] *Milton runs into a flat Thought, sometimes for a hundred Lines together.* Which, I think, is not true: He sometimes flags in many Lines together; and perhaps the same may be as truly said of his Greek Master. In *Homer* methinks I see a Rider of a noble, generous, and fiery Steed; who always puts him upon the Stretch, and therefore sometimes tires him: *Virgil* mounted upon the same, or such another, gives him either the Reins, or the Curb, at proper times; and so his Pace, if not always rapid, as it should not be, is always stately, and majestick; and his Fire appears by being suppressed, as well as by being indulged. For the Judgment of this incomparable Poet, in alternately suppressing, and indulging his Divine Fury, puts me in mind of his own *Apollo* overruling and inspiring his own *Sibyl*; which whole Passage, by the way (for I shall cite but Part of it) is it self one of the noblest Instances of Poetical Fire this Day extant in the whole World. My Application a little perverts it: But That is a small Circumstance in Allusions.

At Phœbi nondum patiens immanis in antro
Bacchatur vates, magnum si pectore possit
Excussisse Deum; tanto magis ille fatigat
Os rabidum, fera corda domans, fingitque premendo.

But afterwards;

Talibus ex adyto dictis Cumæa Sibylla
Horrendas canit ambages, antroque remugit,
Obscuris vera involvens; ea fræna furenti
Concutit, & stimulos sub pectore vertit Apollo.

What was my Lord *Roscommon*'s Precept, was *Virgil*'s Practice,

To write with Fury, but correct with Phlegm:

Things very consistent in their own Nature. And therefore I must insist that *Virgil* was no way deficient in Poetical Fire; and that *Homer* excelled him not in that Particular. By which last I always mean, that either *Homer* had not *more* of it, or if he had *more in the Whole*, he had *too much* in *some* Instances, and *too little* in *others*. If His were *more* than *Virgil*'s, (tho' even That I question) it was not *better*; no nor *so good*: considering how their Fire was disposed, or (if I may so speak) situated in their several Constitutions; and what use they severally made of it in their Writings. And therefore upon this Article I must take the Liberty to say, Mr. *Pope* is not just to *Virgil*, as well as to some other Poets, in the Preface to his admirable Translation of *Homer*. "This Fire (says he) is discerned in *Virgil*; but discerned as through a Glass, reflected, and rather shining than warm, but every-where equal and constant: In *Lucan*, and *Statius*, it bursts out in sudden, short, and interrupted Flashes: In *Milton*, it glows like a Furnace, kept up to an uncommon Fierceness by the Force of Art: In *Shakespear*, it strikes before we are aware, like an accidental Fire from Heaven: But in *Homer*, and in

Him only, it burns every where clearly, and every where irresistibly." Supposing his Account of *Lucan* and *Statius* to be true: I no more know how to distinguish it from his Account of *Shakespear*, than I agree with him in the Character he gives of that great Man. For Fires from Heaven do not *often* strike; and when they do, are of no long Continuance: And so *Shakespear*'s, like That of the other Two before mentioned, is supposed to *burst out in short, sudden, and interrupted Flashes*. For Instance, like Lightning; which is the only Fire from Heaven that we ordinarily see, or hear of, and even That not very frequently. For if any other Celestial flashes are here meant, they indeed may be more Divine; but they are much more rare, and short, than Those of *Statius* and *Lucan*. Whereas *Shakespear*, in my Judgment, has more of the Poetical Fire, than either of those Poets. *Milton* indeed had more of it than He: and therefore I am no less suprized at the Character here given of his Fire, that *it glows like a Furnace, kept up to an uncommon Fierceness by the Force of Art*. Because, tho' his Art, Learning, and Use of Books, especially of *Homer*, be very great; yet he is most distinguished by natural Genius, Spirit, Invention, and Fire; in all which perhaps he is not very much inferiour to *Homer* himself. Whose Fire again does not, I conceive, *burn every where clearly, and irresistibly*: Or if it did, it would be no Commendation. For the small Praise here given to *Virgil*, is, in my Opinion, no true Praise at all: His Fire is not every where equal: and it would be a Fault in him, if it were; as I have above observed. But waving That; Surely such an Account of *Virgil*'s Fire was never given by any Critick before. *It is discerned*: As faint, and lessening an Expression, as could have been thought of. And how is it even *discerned*? Only *through a Glass*: And lest we should imagine That Glass to be a *Burning-Glass*; it is *reflected*, and *rather shining, than warm*. Now I desire to be informed, what truer Idea any one can have of the coldest, and most spiritless Writer in the World; supposing him only to be a good Judge, and a Man of tolerable Parts. If I am my self a little warm upon this Subject, I hope it may be pardoned upon such an Occasion; when so great a Genius as *Virgil*'s is unjustly censured by so great a Genius as Mr. *Pope*'s. However it be; *Homer*, according to this Account, remains the Sun of Poetry: For I know of no other Luminary (to which he may be compared) whose Fire *burns every where clearly, and every where irresistibly*. Whereas, if we must pursue these Similes of Light, and Fire, (tho', like other Similes, they do not answer in every Particular) I should rather say, as I hinted in the Beginning of this Preface, that the Fire of Poetry arose in *Homer*, like Light at the Creation; shining, and burning, it is true, but enshrined in a Cloud: But was afterwards transplanted into *Virgil*, as into the Sun; according to the Account which *Milton* gives of Both:[16]

Let there be Light, said God; and forthwith Light
Ethereal, first of Things, Quintessence pure,
Sprang from the Deep; and from her native East

To journy thro' the airy Gloom began,
Sphear'd in a radiant Cloud: For yet the Sun
Was not; She in a cloudy Tabernacle
Sojourn'd the while.———

Afterwards:

Of Light by far the greater Part he took,
Transplanted from her cloudy Shrine, and plac'd
In the Sun's Orb, made porous to receive
And drink the liquid Light; firm to retain
Her gather'd Beams, great Palace now of Light.

If it be said, that according to this Account, *Homer* has the Advantage; because *all* the Light is supposed to have been first in him, and only a *Part* of it (tho' the greatest) transferred to *Virgil*: it must be remembered that we are only making a *Comparison*: For if it were an exact *Parallel*, we must conceive (which we are far from doing) that the *very individual* Fire of the *Greek* Poet was transferred into the *Roman*; and that the one ceases to exist separately from the other. But besides; admitting *Homer* to have the Advantage *so far* as this Objection supposes; yet still *Virgil* has it *upon the Whole*, even with respect to Fire, of which we are now discoursing. Tho' the Light in the cloudy Shrine were *more* than That in the Sun; yet in the Sun it is placed in a *higher*, and more *regular* Sphere; more *aptly disposed* for *warming* and *illuminating*, and more *commodiously situated* for the Delight and Benefit of Mankind. "The *Roman* Author (we are told) seldom rises into very astonishing Sentiments, where he is not fired by the *Iliad*.[17]" Tho' I absolutely deny the Matter of Fact yet supposing it were true, still *fired he is*: The Poetical Spirit is in him, however he came by it; and that too *better*, if not *more*, than in him from whom he is imagined to have received it. How far the Reader will be of my Opinion upon this Head I know not: But to me the Truth of what I have urged resembles the *Things* of which I have been speaking: It *shines* like the *Light*, and *burns* like the *Fire*.

As to *Similes*, *Homer* is supposed to have the full Propriety of *Them*; and even the greatest Part of *Virgil*'s must be His. That a great Number of *Virgil*'s are taken from him, I deny not; but most of them are exceedingly improved by being transplanted: Tho' I believe if he had taken fewer from *Homer*, and given us more of his own, his Poem would have been so much the better. Not that he really has copy'd from *Homer* in this Instance, near so much as some Criticks pretend; and he has more Similes entirely his own; than the aforesaid Criticks will allow him. In my Remarks I shall mention some Particulars.

Generally speaking, *Homer's Descriptions* are admirable. But even in this View, I think Those are unjust to *Virgil*, who do not allow that he excels his

Master. Consider the several Instances already cited, upon the Article of Poetical Fire; for most of them may be equally applied to This. What Images! what Paintings! what Representations of Nature! what Nature it self, do we find and feel in them! Besides a Multitude of others, which cannot now be so much as mentioned: I must here again refer to my Notes for Particulars.

For *Style*, *Diction*, and *Verification*, *Homer*, I acknowledge, is allowed the Triumph, even by the Generality of *Virgil*'s Party: particularly by *Rapin*; as he is likewise by him in the Instances of *Fire*, and *Description*, above-mentioned. However, that I may not be thought singular in my Opinion, a Character which I by no means desire; it may be considered that I agree with *Scaliger* in his express Assertions, and with my Lord *Roscommon* in his Hints and Insinuations, not to mention other Authorities; when I frankly declare my Sentiments, that the *Roman* Poet is superiour to the *Grecian* even in this Respect. The *Greek* Language, it is true, is superiour to the *Latin*, in This, as well as in every thing else; being the most expressive, the most harmonious, the most various, rich, and fruitful, and indeed, upon all Accounts, the best Language in the World. But if notwithstanding this great Advantage, *Virgil*'s Diction and Versification be preferable to *Homer*'s; his Glory for That very Reason will be so much the greater. *Homer's Epithets*, for the most part, are in *Themselves* exceedingly beautiful; but are not many of them *superfluous*? Whether many, nay all, of those Particles which are commonly (and indeed, I think, falsly enough) called Expletives, be significant or no, I do not now dispute: But admitting them to be so; are not too many little Words, whether *Expletives*, nay whether *Particles*, or not, often crouded together? Ἤ εἰ δή ποτέ τοι κατὰ, &c. and Ἤ ῥά νύ μοί ποτὲ καὶ σὺ, &c. are not, I own, very agreeable Sounds to my Ears; and many more of the same Kind are to be met with. Moreover, does not *Homer* make an ill use of one great Privilege of his Language, (among many others) I mean That of dissolving Diphthongs, by so very frequently inserting a Word of five, or six Syllables, to drag his Sense to the End of a Verse, which concludes with the long Word aforesaid? Those Words, even at the End of a Verse, are sometimes indeed very agreeable: But are they not often otherwise? Especially at the Close of a Paragraph, or Speech; when for the most part too they are Epithets: and yet more especially, when those Epithets are of little Significancy? I shall give but one Instance, tho' it were very easy to produce many; and That shall be the last Line of the *Iliad*: Upon which, compared with the last of the *Æneis*, I cannot but think that

Vitaque cum gemitu fugit indignata sub umbras,

is a nobler Conclusion of an Heroic Poem, than

Ὣς οἵ γ' ἀμφίεπον τάφον Ἕκτορος ἱπποδάμοιο.

A thousand things of the same, or of the like Nature, might be mentioned: And I am aware that such Observations will by some Criticks be called *modern Criticisms*. But be That as it will; I am for Truth and Reason, whether it be called Ancient, or Modern.

To display the Excellence of *Virgil*'s Style, Diction, and Versification, cannot be the Business of this Preface: Here again I must refer to my Notes. I only observe, that nothing can be more sublime, and majestick, than some Parts; nothing more sweet, and soft, than others; nothing more harmonious, flowing, numerous, and sounding than both his Soft, and his Sublime. As to which latter, when he describes the Fury, Noise, and Confusion of War, I recollect That of my Lord *Roscommon*;

Th' Æneian Muse, when she appears in State,
Makes all Jove's *Thunder on her Verses wait.*

And That of *Virgil* himself:

——*Quo non præstantior alter*
Ære ciere viros, Martemque accendere cantu.

For those Lines may as well be applied to the Trumpet of *Virgil*, as of *Misenus*. Not but that in this way of Writing, I mean the Martial, and the Furious, *Homer*, setting aside his Redundancy, is at least equal to *Virgil*; perhaps superiour. But then he is not comparable to him in the other Part, the smooth, the soft, and the sweetly flowing. This in *Virgil* always puts me in mind of some Verses of his own, which I have elsewhere cited: Verses, which, in the Sixth Eclogue, the Speakers apply to each other; and which, above all Writers, are most applicable to Him, who gives Speech to them both.

Tale tuum carmen nobis, divine Poeta,
Quale sopor fessis in gramine, quale per æstum
Dulcis aquæ saliente sitim restinguere rivo.
Nam neque me tantum venientis sibilus Austri,
Nec percussa juvant fluctu tam littora, nec quæ
Saxosas inter decurrunt flumina valles.

But the exquisite Art of *Virgil*'s Versification is seen in his varying the Pauses, and Periods, and Cadence of his Numbers; in being rough or smooth, soft or vehement, long or short, *&c.* according to the Nature of the Ideas he would convey to the Mind: in which, I think, he exceeds all Writers, whether Ancient or Modern; and is in particular the best Versifier, as well as, upon the whole, the best Poet in the World.

Upon the Subject of *Speeches*, Mr. *Pope* tells us, "That in *Virgil* they often consist of general Reflections, or Thoughts, which might be equally just in any Person's Mouth upon the same Occasion. As many of his Persons have no apparent Characters; so many of his Speeches escape being applied, and judged by the Rule of Propriety. We oftner think of the Author himself, when we read *Virgil*, than when we are engaged in *Homer*. All which are the Effects of *a colder Invention*, that interests us less in the Action described: *Homer* makes us Hearers, and *Virgil* leaves us Readers." I have the Misfortune to be of a quite different Sentiment. If *Virgil* outshines *Homer* in any thing, it is especially in his *Speeches*. Which are all, so far as it is necessary, adapted to the Manners of the Speakers, and diversified by their several Characters. Nor do I know of any one Beauty by which *Virgil* is more peculiarly distinguished, than That of his Speeches: Considering the Sweetness and Softness of some, the Cunning and Artifice of others; the Majesty and Gravity of a third sort; the Fire and Fury of a fourth: In which two last Kinds especially we have the united Eloquence of Oratory, and Poetry; and read *Tully* involved in *Virgil*. That the Characters of the Heroes are more particularly marked and distinguished in the *Greek*, than in the *Latin*, I readily acknowledge. In That the *Iliad* excels the *Æneis*; and, I think, in nothing else. And the Controversy between these two great Poets Should, in my Opinion, be thus determined: "That *Virgil* is very much obliged to *Homer*; and *Homer*'s Poems, upon the whole, very much exceeded by *Virgil*'s."

But I am sensible, that by arguing for *Virgil* I have all this while been arguing against my self. For the more excellent the Author, the more presumptuous the Translator. I have however thus much to plead in my Excuse, That this Work was very far *advanced*, before it was *undertaken*; having been for many Years the Diversion of my leisure Hours at the University, and growing upon me by insensible Degrees; so that a great *Part* of the *Æneis* was *actually translated*, before I had *any Design* of *attempting the Whole*. But with regard to the *Publick Office in Poetry*, with which the University of *Oxford* was afterwards pleased to honour me, (an Honour which I Now enjoy, and which I shall Forever gratefully acknowledge) I thought it might not be improper for me to review, and finish this Work; which otherwise had certainly been as much neglected by Me, as perhaps it will now be by Every body else.

It is to That renowned Seat of Learning and Virtue, (the Pride and Glory of our Island!)

———*cujus amor mihi crescit in horas*,

and my Love and Veneration for which I Shall never be able to express: It is to That famous University, I say, that I owe a very considerable Part of my Encouragement in this Undertaking; tho' at the same time I have great and signal Obligations to many *Others*, who were not only Subscribers to it themselves, but Promoters of it by their Interest in their Friends. With the most grateful Sense of the Favour, and Honour done me, I return my *general* Thanks to *All* Those of the Nobility, and Gentry, and all Others, who appear as my Subscribers: But These my *especial Benefactors* are desired to accept of my more *particular* Acknowledgments. Even These (many of whom are Persons of Quality) are so numerous, that to mention them would be to transcribe a great Part of my List into my Preface: And Since I cannot properly name them *All*, I think it the best Manners to name *None*. I wish for Their sakes, as well as my Own, that, when they have read this Translation, they may not repent of the *generous Encouragement* they have given it.

One Thing of which, I hope, I may say; and That is, that *it is a Translation.* And if it be; I believe I may add, that it is almost the only one in Verse, and of a considerable Length. And this I am very far from speaking, upon the Account of any great Opinion which I have conceived of my own Performance. For besides that a Translation may be very *close*, and yet very *bad*. Others could have done the same thing much better, if they would: But they thought it either impracticable, or improper. They have been so averse from the Folly of rendering Word for Word, that they have ran into the other Extreme; and their Translations are commonly so very licentious, that they can scarce be called so much as Paraphrases. Whereas, were it practicable to translate *verbatim* in the strictest Sense; and yet preserve the Elegance, and Sublimity, and Spirit of the Author, as much as if one allowed one's self a greater Latitude: That Method ought to be chosen before the other. And in proportion, the nearer one approaches to the Original, the better it is; provided the Version be in other Respects no way prejudiced, but rather improved by it: A Thing, in my Apprehension, by no Means inconceivable. A Translator should *draw the Picture* of his Author: And in Painting, we know, *Likeness* is the *first* Beauty; so that if it has not *That*, all the rest are insignificant. Draw *Virgil* as *like* as you can; To think of *improving* him is *arrogant*; and to flatter him, is *impossible*. I have not added, or omitted very many Words: Many indeed are varied; the Sense of the Substantive in the Latin, being often transferred to the Adjective in the English; and so on the Reverse: with a great Number of such like Instances, which it is needless to mention. Yet many Lines are translated Word for Word: But, upon the Whole, to give a tolerable, and yet a perfectly litteral Version, I take to be in the Nature of Things absolutely impossible.

I am sensible too, as I said before, that it may be a true Translation, a close Translation; and yet, after all, a very bad Translation. Whether This be so, or not, is with all imaginable Deference submitted to the Judgment of the World. To render the bare Sense, and Words of a Poet, is only to paint his Features, and Lineaments; but to render his *Poetry*, that is, the *peculiar Turn* of his Thoughts, and Diction, is to paint his *Air* and *Manner*. And as the Air of a Face arises from a Man's *Soul*, as well as from his Body; it is just the same here: Or rather, This peculiar Turn of the Poet's Sentiments and Expressions *is it self* the Soul of his Poetry: If we are asked what That is; the Answer must be, if we may properly compare a *Mode* to a *Substance*, that the Soul of Poetry, like the Soul of Man, is perceivable only by its Effects; like That, immaterial, and invisible; and like That too, immortal.

But then all this being taken care of, certainly the nearer to the Original, the better: Nay indeed it is impossible to hit the Air right; unless you hit the Features, from which the Air, so far as it relates to the Body, rises, and results. Should my Translation be approved of for the Spirit of Poetry; I should not be sorry, nay I should be glad, if at the same time it served for a Construing-Book to a School-Boy. But still whenever it happens (as it very often does, and must) that a close Version, and a graceful Expression are inconsistent; the latter is always to be preferred. A *less litteral Translation* is very frequently beautiful; but nothing can justify *an ill Verse*. In This Case, one departs from the Original by adhering to it; and such an Author as *Virgil* might justly say of his bad Translator, what *Martial* says of his bad Neighbour;

Nemo tam prope, tam proculque nobis.

For the Version would retain more not only of the *Beauty*, but of the *real Sense* of the Original; and so *upon the whole*, be more *like* it: If it were a less faithful Interpretation of Words and Expressions.

Here therefore we can no longer pursue the Comparison between Painting and Translating: When true Beauty is to be imitated, the Features cannot be too exactly traced in the One, to make a handsom Likeness; but Words may be too exactly rendered in the Other. Upon this Head I cannot avoid transcribing a Passage from the ingenious, and (in all Instances, but one) judicious Dr. *Felton*'s Dissertation upon *Reading the Classicks addressed to the Lord Marquis of* Granby. "When therefore ([18]says He) you meet with any Expressions which will not be rendered without this Disadvantage, the Thing to be regarded is the Beauty and Elegance of the Original; and your Lordship, without minding any thing but the Sense of the Author, is to consider how that Passage would be best expressed in *English*, if you were not tied up to the Words of the Original: And you may depend upon it, that if you can find a Way of expressing the same Sense as beautifully in *English*; you have hit the true Translation, tho' you cannot construe the Words backwards, and forwards into one another: For then you certainly have translated, as the Author, were he an *Englishman*, would have wrote." And since I have cited thus much from That Treatise; I will borrow a little more from it upon the Nature, and Difficulty of Translations in general: Because it entirely expresses my Sentiments, in far better Words than I am able to make use of. "[19]'Tis no exceeding Labour for every great Genius to exert, and manage, and master his own Spirit: But 'tis almost an insuperable Task to compass, to equal, to command the Spirit of another Man. Yet this is what every Translator taketh upon himself to do; and must do, if he deserves the Name. He must put himself into the Place of his Authors, not only be Master of their Manner as to their Style, their Periods, Turn, and Cadence of their Writings; but he must bring himself to their Habit, and Way of Thinking, and have, if possible, the same Train of Notions in his Head, which gave Birth to Those they have selected, and placed in their Works." For the Rest, I refer my Reader to the Dissertation it self; of which I would say that it is a most curious and delicate Piece of Wit, and Criticism, and polite Learning; did I not fear that (for a Reason which I will not mention) it would look like Vanity in Me to do common Justice to it's Author. At the same time I must acknowledge that the Doctor represents a Translation of *Virgil* after Mr. *Dryden*'s as a desperate Undertaking: Which would be no small Mortification to me; were not mine of a different Nature from His: Of which more in it's proper Place.

Endeavouring to resemble *Virgil* as much as possible, I have imitated him in his *Breaks*. For tho' I am satisfied he never intended to leave those Verses unfinished, and therefore he is in that Particular absurdly mimicked by some Moderns in their Original Writings; yet *unfinished they are*. And this Imitation is not (with Mr. *Dryden*'s Leave) "like the Affectation of *Alexander*'s Courtiers, who held their Necks awry, because He could not help it." For besides that a *wry Neck* is one thing, and a *Scar* is another; *Apelles* in a *Picture* ought to have imitated his Master's Imperfection, if he intended to draw an exact Likeness, tho' his *Courtiers* were ridiculous Flatterers for doing the Same in their *Gestures*.

A Work of This Nature is to be regarded in Two different Views; both as a *Poem*, and as a *Translated Poem*. In the one, all Persons of good Sense, and a true Taste of Poetry, are Judges of it; tho' they are skilled in no Language, but their Own. In the other, Those only are so; who besides the Qualification just mentioned, are familiarly acquainted with the Original. And it may well admit of a Question, to which of these Species of Readers a good Translation is the more agreeable Entertainment. The Unlearned are affected like Those, who see the Picture of One whose Character they admire; but whose Person they never saw: The Learned, like Those who see the Picture of one whom they love, and admire; and with whom they are intimately acquainted. The Reason of the first Pleasure is clear; but That of the last requires a little more Consideration. It may all, be resolved into the Love of Imitation, Comparison, and Variety; which arises from the Imperfection of human Happiness; for a Reason which I have elsewhere[20] assigned. Delightful therefore it is to compare the Version with the Original: Through the whole Course of which Comparison, we discover many retired Beauties in the Author himself, which we never before observed. Delightful it must be to have the same Ideas started in our Minds, different ways; and the more agreeable those Ideas are in themselves, the more agreeable is this Variety. Therefore, the better we understand a Poet, the more we love and admire him; the more Pleasure we conceive in reading him well translated: As we most delight to see the Pictures of Those whom we best love; and to see the Persons themselves in Variety of Dresses. Upon which Account, I will be bold to affirm; that he who says he values no Translation of this, or that Poem, because he understands the Original, has indeed no true Relish, that is, in effect, no *true Understanding* of *Either*.

It is indeed no less certain on the Reverse, that a Man is as much provoked to see an ill Picture of his Friend, or Mistress, as he is pleased to see a good one; and it is just the same in Translations. But it is evident that the *bare Understanding* of a Poet (as that Word is commonly used) is not the *only* Argument of one's *truly* understanding him: that is, understanding him as a *Poet*. Because what I have just now said, concerning the Agreeableness of a good Translation, holds as true, when it is from our own Language to another, as when it is from another to our own. It may be presumed that *Milton*'s *Paradise Lost*, being in *English*, is well *understood* (vulgarly speaking) by *Englishmen*. But notwithstanding That, were it possible (as I think it is not) to have all That amazing Poem as well translated into *Latin*, or *Greek*, as some Parts of it certainly may be; with what Pleasure should we read it! And he who would not read such a Translation with Pleasure, will, I believe, be allowed by all who have a right Taste of Poetry not *truly* to understand the Original. Besides what I have said concerning the Delight arising from Imitation, Comparison, and Variety, which respects the Relation between the Version, and the Original; the Translator's Work, even to Those who understand the Original, is in a great measure a *New Poem*. The Thought, and Contrivance are his Author's; but his Language, and the Turn of his Versification, and Expressions, are his own. What I have offered upon this Subject relates to Translations in general: Of my own in particular I have nothing to say, but what I have said before; which is to submit it to the Judgment of Others.

In Pursuance of my Design of endeavouring to be as like *Virgil* as possible; I have chosen Blank Verse, rather than Rhime. For besides that the Fetters of Rhime often cramp the Expression, and spoil the Verse, and so you can both translate more closely, and also more fully express the Spirit of your Author, without it, than with it; I say besides This, supposing other Circumstances were equal, Blank Verse is *in it self better*. It is not only more

Majestick, and Sublime, but more Musical, and Harmonious: It has more *Rhime* in it, according to the ancient, and true Sense of the Word, than Rhime it self, as it is now used. For in it's original Signification, it consists not in the Tinkling of Vowels, and Consonants; but in the metrical Disposition of Words, and Syllables, and the proper Cadence of Numbers; which is more agreeable to the Ear, without the Jingling of like Endings, than with it. The Reader may say, To whose Ear is it so? To Yours perhaps; but not to Mine. And I grant all This to be matter of Fact, rather than of Reason; and to be determined by Votes, rather than Arguments. And accordingly a great Majority of the best Genius's, and Judges in Poetry now living, with many of whom I have frequently conversed upon this Subject, have determined in favour of this way of Writing. And among Those who are dead, the same was the Opinion not only of my Lord *Roscommon* (to omit others,) but of [21]Mr. *Dryden* Himself; who was the best Rhimer, as well as the best Poet, of the Age in which he lived. And indeed let but a Man consult his own Ears.

——*Him the Almighty Pow'r*
Hurl'd headlong, flaming from th' ethereal Sky,
With hideous Ruin, and Combustion, down
To bottomless Perdition; there to dwell
In Adamantine Chains, and penal Fire;
Who durst defy th' Omnipotent to Arms.
Nine times the Space that measures Day, and Night
To mortal Men, he with his horrid Crew
Lay vanquish'd, rowling in the fiery Gulph,
Confounded, tho' immmortal——

Who that hears This, can think it wants Rhime to recommend it? Or rather does not think it sounds far better without it? I purposely produced a Citation, beginning and ending in the Middle of a Verse; because the Privilege of resting on this, or that Foot, sometimes one, and sometimes another, and so diversifying the Pauses, and Cadences, is the greatest Beauty of Blank Verse, and perfectly agreeable to the Practice of our Masters, the *Greeks*, and *Romans*. This can be done but rarely in Rhime: For if it were frequent, the Rhime would be, in a manner, lost by it: The End of almost every Verse must be something of a Pause; and it is but seldom that a Sentence begins in the Middle. The same may be said of placing the Verb after the Accusative Case; and the Adjective after the Substantive; both which, especially the last, are more frequent in Blank Verse, than in Rhime. This Turn of Expression likewise is agreeable to the Practice of the Ancients; and even in our own Language adds much to the Grandeur, and Majesty of the Poem, if it be wrought with Care, and Judgment. As does also the judicious interspersing (for *judicious*, and *sparing* it must be) of *antique* Words, and of such as, being derived from *Latin*, retain the Air of That Language: Both which have a better Effect in Blank Verse, than in Rhime; by Reason of a certain Majestick Stiffness, which becomes the one, more than the other. *Milton* indeed has, I think, rather too much of This: And perhaps the most ingenious Mr. *Philips* has too much imitated him in it; as he has certainly well nigh equalled him in his most singular Beauties. I speak of this Stiffness only in some particular Passages, for which it is proper: For Blank Verse, when it pleases, can be as smooth, as soft, and as flowing, as Rhime. Now these Advantages alone (were there no other) which Blank Verse has above Rhime, would more than compensate for the Loss of that Pleasure which comes from the Chiming of Syllables; the former, by reason of those Advantages, being, all things considered, even more musical, and harmonious, as well as more noble, and sublime, than the latter.

Upon Varying the Pauses it is to be observed, that Two Verses together should rarely pause at the same Foot; for a Reason too plain to be mentioned. I said *rarely*; because there is no Law so strict in Things of This Nature, but that it is sometimes a Vertue to break it. And tho' it be one great Privilege in this sort of Verse, to make a full Period at the Beginning, or in the Middle of a Line; yet you may do it too often. *Milton*, I think, does so; who sometimes gives you thirty, or forty Verses together, not one of which concludes with a full Period. But to return to our Comparison.

Tho' all This be rather Matter of Sense, than of Reason; yet I appealed to the best Genius's, and Judges in Poetry; because it is a great Mistake to think that all Ears are equally Judges. It may as well, nay better, be affirmed that all Persons have equally Ears for Musick. This Sentiment is not *purely* Organical, and depends not *solely* upon the Mechanism of Sense. The Judgment has *a Share* in it: Or if it has not; there is (which amounts to much the same) so close an Union between the Soul and Body of Man, as also between the Spirit and the Diction, which may be called the Soul and Body of Poetry; that the Poetical Turn of any Person's Mind affects the very Organs of Sense. Readers of vulgar and mean Tastes may relish Rhime best; and so may Some even of the best Taste; because they have been habituated to it. But the more they accustom themselves to Blank Verse; the better they will like it:

————*Si propius stes,*
Te capiet magis————

After all, I cannot agree with Those, who *entirely condemn* the Use of Rhime even in an Heroic Poem; nor can I absolutely reject That in Speculation, which Mr. *Dryden*, and Mr. *Pope* have ennobled by their Practice. I acknowledge too that, in some particular Views, tho' not upon the Whole,

This Way of Writing has the Advantage over the other. You may pick out more Lines, which, singly considered, look mean, and low, from a Poem in Blank Verse, than from one in Rhime: supposing them to be in other respects equal. Take the Lines singly by themselves, or in Couplets; and more in Blank Verse shall be less strong, and smooth, than in Rhime: But then take a considerable Number together; and Blank Verse shall have the Advantage in both Regards. Little, and ignoble Words, as *Thus, Now, Then, Him*, &c. on the one Hand; and long ones, as *Elements, Omnipotent, Majesty*, &c. on the other, would in a Poem consisting of Rhime sound weak, and languishing, at the End of a Verse: because the Rhime draws out the Sound of those Words, and makes them observed, and taken notice of by the Ear: Whereas in Blank Verse they are covered, and concealed by running immediately into the next Line. And yet a considerable Number of Lines are not, in the Main, Prosaick, or Flat; but more Noble, than if they were all in Rhime. For Instance, the following Verses out of *Milton's Paradise Lost*, Book II.

Of Heav'n were falling, and these Elements——

Instinct with Fire, and Nitre hurry'd him——

taken singly, look low, and mean; but pray read them in Conjunction with others; and then see what a different Face will be set upon them.

——Or less than if this Frame
Of Heav'n were falling, and these Elements
In Mutinie had from her Axle torn
The stedfast Earth. At last his sail-broad Vans
He spreads for flight; and in the surging Smoke, &c.

——Had not by ill chance
The strong Rebuff of some tumultuous Cloud
Instinct with Fire, and Nitre, hurry'd him
As many miles aloft. That fury stay'd;
Quench'd in a boggy Syrtis, neither Sea,
Nor good dry Land: Nigh founder'd on he fares,
Treading the crude Consistence——

Thus again in the VIth Book.

Had to her Center shook. What wonder? when——

Had not th' Eternal King Omnipotent——

And limited their Might; tho' number'd such——

These Verses disjointed from their Fellows make but an indifferent Figure: But read the following Passage and I believe you will acknowledge there is not one bad Verse in it:

So under fiery Cope together rush'd
Both Battles maine, with ruinous Assault,
And inextinguishable Rage: All Heav'n
Resounded; and had Earth been then, all Earth
Had to her Center shook. What wonder? when
Millions of fierce encountring Angels fought
On either side; the least of whom could wield
These Elements, and arm him with the force
Of all their Regions. How much more of pow'r,
Army 'gainst Army, numberless, to raise
Dreadful Combustion, warring, and disturb,
Tho' not destroy, their happy native Seat:
Had not th' Eternal King Omnipotent
From his strong Hold of Heav'n high over-rul'd
And limited their Might; tho' number'd such
As each divided Legion might have seem'd
A num'rous Host in strength, each armed hand
A Legion——

In Short, a Poem consisting of Rhime is like a Building in which the Stones are all (or far the greatest part of them) *hewn with equal Exactness*; but are all of a Shape, and not so well jointed: *Every one* of them, *by it self*, is better squared, than *some* in another Building, in which they are of different Figures. But tho' in this latter there shall be a few, which, taken separately, do not look so well: yet some *running into others*, and all being *better adjusted* together; it shall not only *upon the Whole*, but with regard to any *considerable Part*, by it self, be a stronger, and a more beautiful Fabrick, than the former.

But we are told that Blank Verse is not enough distinguished from Prose. The Answer must be, It is according as it is. That of our *English* Tragedies, I confess, is not; tho' very proper for the Purpose to which it is apply'd. This indeed is what the *French* rightly call *Prose mesurée*, rather than Verse. But much worse is to be said of *any* Poem, which is only written in the Shape of Metre, but has no more of Verse in it, than of Rhime; no Harmony, or Prosody, no true Metrical Cadence; half the Lines concluding with double Syllables, as *Torment, Greatness*, and the Participles ending in *ing*. This deserves not so much as the Name of *Prose on Horseback*; 'Tis Prose upon Crutches; and of all Prose the vilest. But if Blank Verse be laboured, as it ought to be; it is sufficiently distinguished from Prose. We have no Feet, nor Quantities, like the Ancients; and nothing in our poor Language will ever supply That Defect: Rhime is at least as far from doing it, as the more

Advantageous Variety of Cadences in Blank Verse: Which requires so much the more Care, and Art, to work it up into Numbers, and Support it from groveling into Prose.

Which naturally leads us to observe further, that many Imperfections, both in Thought, and Expression, will be overlooked in Rhime, which will not be endured in Blank Verse: So that the same may be said of This, which *Horace* applies to Comedy;

Creditur———habere
Sudoris minimum; sed habet———tanto
Plus oneris, quanto veniæ minus———

I do not say, Rhime is, all things considered, more easy than the other: That Point cannot be well determined; because it relates to the particular Genius's of particular Persons. For my own part, if I never made one good Verse, I have made many good Rhimes: But supposing Both to be equally easy, I should chuse Blank Verse, for the Reasons already alledged.

After all which, if some Gentlemen are resolved that *Blank Verse shall* be *Prose*; they have my free Leave to *enjoy their Saying*: provided I may have Theirs to think they mean nothing by it; unless they can prove that Rhime is essential to Metre; consequently that the *Goths*, and *Monks* were the first Inventers of Verse; and that *Homer*, and *Virgil*, as well as *Milton*, wrote nothing but Prose.

Milton indeed has *too many* of those looser and weaker Verses; as he has some Lines which are no Verses at all. These for Instance,

Burnt after them to the bottomless Pit:

In the Visions of God; It was a Hill:

are Lines consisting of ten Syllables; but they are no more *English* Verses, than they are *Greek* ones. Many *irregular* and *redundant* Verses, and more of an ill Sound and Cadence, are to be met with in his Poem; sometimes a considerable Number of them together. Whether This was *Negligence* in him, or *Choice*, I know not. Certain it is from the main Tenour of his Verification, than which nothing can be more heroically sonorous, that it was not Want of Ear, Genius, or Judgment. What is the true Cadence of an *English* Verse, is sufficiently known to the Ears of every one who has a Taste of Poetry. Sometimes it is not only allowable, but beautiful, to run into harsh, and unequal Numbers. Mr. *Dryden* himself does it; and we may be sure he knew when he did it, as well as we could tell him. In a Work intended for Pleasure, *Variety* justifies the Breach of almost any Rule, provided it be done but *rarely*. Among the Ancient Poets, what are many of those *Figures* (as we call them) both in Prosody, and Syntax, but so many

Ways of making *false Quantity*, and *false Grammar*, for the sake of *Variety*? False, I mean, ordinarily speaking; for Variety, and That only, makes it elegant. *Milton* however has too much irregular Metre: But if his overruling Genius, and Merit might in Him *authorize* it, or at least *excuse* it; yet *nobis non licet esse tam audacibus*: especially when I am translating *Virgil*, the most exact, and accurate Versificator in the World: A Character, however, which he would not deserve (for the Reason just mentioned) were he not in *some* Verses irregular, and unaccurate. I am sure I have truly imitated him in *That*; I wish I may have done so in *any thing else*.

Two Things remain to be taken notice of, equally relating to Rhime, and Blank Verse. It is a known Fault in our Language, that it is too much crouded with *Monosyllables*: Yet some Verses consisting wholly of them sound well enough: However, the fewer we have of them, the better it is. I believe there are as few of them in this Translation as in any *English* Poem of an equal Length; which is all I shall say upon This Article.

The Other is the *Elision of Vowels*: Upon which, in my Opinion, the Criticks have ran into Extremes on both Sides. Mr. *Dryden* declares for it as a general Rule which he has observed without Exception, in his Translation of the *Æneis*;[22] and is utterly against *a Vowel gaping after another for want of a Cesura*, as he expresses himself. Another great Master and Refiner of our Language[23] is for very little, or no Abbreviation; if I do not mistake his Meaning. It is true, in the Letter, to which I refer, he instances only in cutting off the Vowel E at the End of our Participles ending in *ed*; but I presume his Argument is equally designed against the Elision of a Vowel before a Vowel in two different Words: And, if I do not forget, he has declared himself of That Opinion, when I have had the Honour and Pleasure of his most agreeable and instructive Conversation. But with humble Submission to both these great Men, the Elision seems sometimes proper, and sometimes not, in the Particle *The*; for upon That, and the Particle *To*, the Question chiefly turns; *He*, and *She* being but very rarely abbreviated by any tolerable Writer: And therefore Mr. *Dryden* expresses himself too much at large, when he speaks of Vowels in general. And when this Elision is proper, and when not, the Ear is a sufficient Judge. The *French*, we know, continually use it in their *Le*, and that in Prose, and common Discourse, as well as in Verse: *L'Amour, L'Eternel, L'Invincible*, &c. As also in their Pronouns, *me, te*, and *se*. In our *English* Poetry, I think it may be either, *Th' Eternal, Th' Almighty*; or *The Eternal, The Almighty*; but rather the former: It should be always, *The Army, The Enemy*; never *Th' Army*, or *Th' Enemy*. And so in other Instances: Of which the Ear (which by the way will never endure the Sound of *Th' Ear*) is always to be Judge. But of these Things too much.

The Kind of Verse therefore, which I have chosen, distinguishes this Translation from Those of Others, who have gone before me in this bold Undertaking: For I had never heard of Dr. *Brady*'s Design, 'till long after This was in a great Forwardness. And His being not yet executed; He is not to be reckoned among my Predecessors: of whom I presume it is expected that I should now give some Account. When I say my Translation is thus distinguished from Those of Others, I speak of our own Countrymen; because *Hannibal Caro*'s *Italian Æneis* is in Blank Verse, such as it is: For [24]Mr. *Dryden*'s Character of it is a very true one; and I need not add any thing to it. Few Persons were ever more familiarly acquainted with the *Æneis*, had a truer Gust, and Relish of it's Beauties, or enter'd more deeply into the Sentiments, into the very Soul, and Spirit of it's Author, than Monsieur *Segrais*. His Preface is altogether admirable; and his Translation perhaps almost as good as the *French* Language will allow; which is just as fit for an Epic Poem, as an ambling Nag is for a War-Horse. It is indeed my Opinion of the *French*; that none write better *of* Poetry, and few (as to *Metre*) worse *in* it. Their Language is excellent for Prose; but quite otherwise for Verse, especially Heroic. And therefore tho' the Translating of Poems into Prose is a strange, modern Invention; yet the *French* Transposers are in the right; because their Language will not bear Verse. The Translation of the *Æneis* into *Scotish* Metre by *Gawin Douglas* Bishop of *Donkeld*, is said to be a very extraordinary Work by Those who understand it better than I do: There being added to it a long List of great Men, who give him a wonderful Character, both as an excellent Poet, and a most pious Prelate. What Mr. *Pope* says of *Ogilby's Homer*, may as well be apply'd to his *Virgil*, that his Poetry is too mean for Criticism. Mr. *Dryden* tells us, that no Man understood *Virgil* better than the Earl of *Lauderdale*; and I believe few did. His Translation is pretty near to the Original; tho' not so close, as it's Brevity would make one imagine; and it sufficiently appears that he had a right Taste of Poetry in general, and of *Virgil's* in particular. He shews a true Spirit; and in many Places is very beautiful. But we should certainly have seen *Virgil* far better translated by a Noble Hand; had the Earl of *Lauderdale* been the Earl of *Roscommon*; or had the *Scotish* Peer followed all the Precepts, and been animated with the Genius of the *Irish*.

But the most difficult, and invidious Part of my prefacing Task is yet to come. How could I have the Confidence to attempt a Translation of *Virgil*, after Mr. *Dryden*? At least to publish it; after Mr. *Pope* has in effect given us his Opinion before-hand, that such a Work must be unsuccessful to any Undertaker (much more to so mean a one, as I am) by declaring that *He* would never undertake it *Himself*? I do not say he makes That Inference; but if his *Modesty* would not suffer him to do it, his *Merit* must oblige others to do it for him. I so far agree with That most ingenious Gentleman, that Mr. *Dryden*'s is, in many Parts, a noble, and spirited Translation; and yet I cannot, upon the Whole, think it a good one; at least, for Mr. *Dryden*. Not but that I think his Performance is prodigious, and exceedingly for his Honour, considering the little time he allowed himself for so mighty a Work; having translated not the *Æneis* only, but all *Virgil's* Poems in the Compass of three Years. Nobody can have a truer Respect for That great Man, than I have; or be more ready to defend him against his unreasonable Accusers; who (as Mr. *Pope* justly observes) envy, and calumniate him. But I hope I shall not be thought guilty of either (I am sure they are the Things of the World which I abhor) if I presume to say that his Writings have their dark, as well as their bright Side; and that what was said of somebody else may be as well applied to Him: *Ubi bene, nemo melius; Ubi male, nemo pejus.*

This may be affirmed of his Works in general; but I am now obliged to consider his Translation of the *Æneis* in particular. As he was the great Refiner of our *English* Poetry, and the best Marshaller of Words that our Nation had then, at least, produced; and all, who have followed him, are extremely indebted to him, as such: his Versification here, as every where else, is generally flowing, and harmonious; and a multitude of Beauties of all kinds are scattered through the Whole. But then, besides his often grosly mistaking his Author's Sense; as a Translator, he is extremely licentious. Whatever he alledges to the contrary in his Preface; he makes no Scruple of adding, or retrenching, as his Turn is best served by either. In many Places, where he shines most as a Poet, he is least a Translator; And where you most admire Mr. *Dryden*, you see least of *Virgil*. Then whereas my Lord *Roscommon* lays down this just Rule to be observed by a Translator with regard to his Author,

Fall, as he falls; and as he rises, rise:

Nothing being more absurd than for those two Counter-parts to be like a Pair of Scales, one mounting as the other sinks; Mr. *Dryden* frequently acts contrary to this Precept, at least to the latter Part of it: Where his *Author* soars, and towers in the Air, *He* often grovels, and flutters upon the Ground. Instances of all these Kinds are numerous. If I produce a few, it is not to detract from his Translation, in order to recommend my own: I detest That base Principle of little, and envious Spirits: And besides, I am sensible that it would be as foolish, as ungenerous: For of Mine, the World *will,* and *ought to be* judge, whatever I say, or think; and it's Judgment in these Matters is never erroneous. It is not therefore that I am acted by the Spirit of *malevolent* Criticism, or Criticism *commonly so called*; which is nothing but the Art of finding Fault: But I do it, partly to *justify* my *Undertaking* (tho' of a different Kind from His, which is what I *chiefly* insist upon) not to *recommend* my *Performance*; partly for the Instruction, and Improvement of my self, and others; for the sake of Truth, and *true Criticism*; that is, right, and impartial Judgment, joined with good Nature, and good Manners; prone to *excuse,* but not to *falsify*; and *delighting* to dwell upon *Beauties*, tho' *daring* to remark upon *Faults*.

Were we to make a few scattered Strictures upon the First Book only; we should observe that he leaves out a very material Word in the very *first* Line: And That too happens to be the Word *First*: As if That stood for Nothing, in *Virgil*'s Verse; and as if *First* would not have stood as well as *Forc'd* in his own. Especially, since there are two Adjectives more of the same Signification [*Expell'd*, and *Exil'd* in the next Verse but one] agreeing with the same Substantive, all three to express the single Epithet *Profugus*. Which, by the way, is Tautology, and utterly unlike *Virgil*'s Manner; who never says any thing in vain, and whose chief Beauty is Brevity. In the very next two Lines, *Italiam, Lavinaque Littora* are left out; tho' necessary to the Design of the Poem: Not to mention his strange Transposing of *sævæ memorem Junonis ob iram*. V. 28. *Long cited by the People of the Sky*, is entirely added. As is, V. 41. *Electra's Glories, and her injur'd Bed*; and the two following Lines. The Addition of three Verses together is too much in all Reason. V. 66. *Then as an Eagle grasps the trembling Game*, is wholly his own. And so is V. 107, 108. *The charming Daughters of the Main Around my Person wait, and bear my Train*. V. 144, 145.——*Whose dismember'd Hands yet bear The Dart aloft, and clench the pointed Spear*. As there is no Hint of This in *Virgil*; so I doubt it is not Sense in it self. For how the Hand of a Body, which has been dead seven Years, can hold a Spear aloft, I cannot imagine. V. 220. *And quenches their innate Desire of Blood*. This is not only added; but too gross, and horrid for *Virgil*'s Meaning in that Place. V. 233. After, *Two Rows of Rocks* (which, by the way, is no Translation of *geminique minantur in cœlum scopuli*) the next Words are totally omitted; *Quorum sub vertice late Æquora tuta silent*. V. 459. *Then on your Name shall wretched Mortals call*, is not included in *Multa tibi ante aras nostra cadet hostia dextra*. He is speaking of *himself*, and his *Friends* in particular; not of *wretched Mortals* in general; of *Thanksgiving*, not of *Prayer*. V. 886.——*You shall find, If not a costly Welcome, yet a kind*, is no more in *Virgil*, than it is like his Stile. But as for the *Flatnesses*, and low *prosaick* Expressions, which are not a few, and which even the Rhime neither covers, nor excuses; I will for several Reasons forbear to transcribe any of them. These *Errata* which I have mentioned in the First Book only, (and there are in it many more such, which I have not mentioned) are either in *adding to*, or *curtailing*, or *mistaking* the Sense of the Original.

But upon the Article of adding to his Author, and altering his Sense, there is one Fault in Mr. *Dryden* which is not to be pardoned. I mean when he does it directly contrary not only to the *Sense*, but to the *Temper* and *Genius* of his Author; and that too in those Instances which injure him not only as a *good Poet*, but as a *good Man*. As *Virgil* is the most chaste, and modest of

Poets, and has ever the strictest Regard to Decency; after the Prayer of *Iarbas* to *Jupiter* in the Fourth Book, he proceeds thus:

Talibus orantem dictis, arasque tenentem
Audiit omnipotens; oculosque ad mœnia torsit
Regia, & oblitos famæ melioris amantes.

What could be more well-mannered, more delicate, and truly *Virgilian*, than the Sweetness, and Softness of that remote, insinuating Expression, *oblitos famæ melioris amantes*? For this Piece of a Verse Mr. *Dryden* gives us Three entire ones; which I will not transcribe. The two first are totally his own; and to One who is not himself *insensible of Shame*, those fulsom Expressions must be very nauseous. Part of the last Verse indeed is *Virgil*'s; and it comes in strangely, after the odious Stuff that goes before it. If *Virgil* can be said to be remarkable for any one good Quality more than for Modesty, it is for his awful Reverence to Religion. And yet, as Mr. *Dryden* represents him describing *Apollo*'s Presence at one of his own Festivals, he speaks Thus; Book iv. V. 210.

Himself, on Cynthus walking, sees below
The merry Madness of the sacred Show.

Virgil says, He walks on the Top of *Cynthus*; That's all: The rest is Mr. *Dryden*'s. And it is exactly of a Piece with a Passage in the Third Georgick; in which, without any sort of Provocation, or the least Hint from his Author, He calls the *Priest* the *Holy Butcher.* If Mr. *Dryden* took Delight in abusing Priests, and Religion; *Virgil* did not. It is indeed wonderful that a Man of so fine, and elevated a Genius, and at the same time of so good a Judgment, as Mr. *Dryden* certainly was, could so much as endure those clumsey Ideas, in which he perpetually rejoices; and that to such a degree, as to thrust them into *Translations*, contrary not only to the Design, and Meaning, but even to the Spirit, and Temper, and most distinguishing Character of his Author. Thus in his Translation of the last Lines of *Homer*'s First Iliad he describes the Gods, and Goddesses as being drunk; and that in no fewer than three Verses, and in some of the coarsest Expressions that our Language will admit of: Whereas the Original gives not the least Intimation of any such thing; but only says that they were *sleepy*, and went *to bed.* And therefore here again I cannot be of Mr. *Pope*'s Opinion, *that it is a great Loss to the Poetical World that Mr.* Dryden *did not live to translate the Iliad.* If we may judge of what the Whole would have been by the Specimen which he has left us; I think it was a Gain to the Poetical World that Mr. *Dryden*'s Version did not hinder us from Mr. *Pope*'s. Which may be said, without any great Compliment to the latter.

As to the Instances of Mr. *Dryden*'s sinking, where his Author most remarkably rises, and being flat where his Author is most remarkably elegant; they are many: But I am almost tired with Quotations; quite tired with such invidious ones, as these are; it being (as I said) much more agreeable to my Temper to remark upon Beauties, than upon Faults, and Imperfections; especially in the Works of great Men, who (tho' they may have written many things not capable of being defended, yet) have written many more, which I can only admire, but do not pretend to equal. And That is the present Case. I shall therefore mention but one Example of this Kind; And it is the unutterable Elegancy of these Lines in the Fourth Book, describing the Scrietch-Owl:

Solaque culminibus, ferali carmine bubo
Sæpe queri, & *longas in fletum ducere voces.*

How is This translated in the following Verses? Or rather is it translated at all?

———With a boding Note
The solitary Scrietch-Owl strains her Throat;
And on a Chimney's Top, or Turret's height,
With Songs obscene disturbs the Silence of the Night.

To produce more Instances would be needless; because One general Remark supersedes them all. It is acknowledged by every body that the First Six Books in the Original are the best, and the most perfect; but the Last Six are so in Mr. *Dryden*'s Translation. Not that even in These *Virgil* properly sinks, or flags in his Genius; but only he did not live to correct them, as he did the former. However, they abound with Beauties in the Original; and so indeed they do in the Translation, more, as I said, than the First Six: Which is visible to any one that reads the Whole with Application.

I observed in the last place, that where Mr. *Dryden* shines most, we often see least of *Virgil*. To omit many other Instances, the Description of the *Cyclops* forging Thunder for *Jupiter*, and Armour for *Æneas*, is elegant, and noble to the last degree in the *Latin*; and it is so to a very great degree in the *English*. But then is the *English* a Translation of the *Latin*?

Hither the Father of the Fire by Night
Thro' the brown Air precipitates his Flight:
On their eternal Anvils here be found
The Brethren beating, and the Blows go round.

Our Language, I think, will admit of few things more truly Poetical, than those four Lines. But the two first are set to render

Huc tunc Ignipotens cœlo descendit ab alto.

There is nothing of *cœlo ab alto* in the Version; nor of *by Night, brown Air,* or *precipitates his Flight* in the Original. The two last are put in the room of

Ferrum exercebant vasto Cyclopes in antro,
Brontesque, Steropesque, & nudus membra Pyracmon.

Vasto in antro in the first of these Lines, and the last Line entirely are left out in the Translation. Nor is there any thing of *eternal Anvils* (I wish there were) or *here be found*, in the Original: And *the Brethren beating, and the Blows go round*, is but a loose Version of *Ferrum exercebant*. Much the same may be said of the whole Passage throughout; which will appear to Those who compare the *Latin* with the *English*. In the whole Passage Mr. *Dryden* has the true Spirit of *Virgil*; but he would have had never the less of it, if he had more closely adhered to his Words, and Expressions.

Sometimes he is *near enough* to the Original; And tho' he *might have been nearer*, he is altogether admirable, not only as a *Poet*, but as a *Translator*. Thus in the Second Book;

Pars ingentem formidine turpi
Scandunt rursus equum, & nota conduntur in alvo.

And some, oppress'd with more ignoble Fear,
Remount the hollow Horse, and pant in secret there.

And in the Twelfth, after the last Speech of *Juturna*;

Tantum effata, caput glauco contexit amictu,
Multa gemens, & se fluvio Dea condidit alto.

She drew a length of Sighs; no more she said,
But with her azure Mantle wrap'd her Head;
Then plung'd into her Stream with deep Despair,
And her last Sobs came bubbling up in Air.

Tho' the last Line is not expressed in the Original, yet it is in some measure imply'd; and it is in it self so exceedingly beautiful, that the whole Passage can never be too much admired. These are Excellencies indeed; This is truly Mr. *Dryden*. *Si sic omnia dixisset*, tho' he had approached no nearer to the Original than This; my other Criticisms upon his Translation had been spared. And after all, I desire that Mine, being in a different sort of Verse, may be considered as an Undertaking of *another kind*, rather than as an Attempt to *excel His*. For tho' I think even That may very well *be done*; yet I am too sensible of my own Imperfection, to presume to say it can be done by *Me*. I have nothing to plead, besides what I have already alledged, in Excuse of my many, and great Faults, in the Execution of This bold Design; but that I was drawn into it, not by any Opinion of my Abilities to perform it, but by the inexpressible Passion which I have always had for this incomparable Poet. With a View to whom, I will here insert a noble

Stroke out of my Lord *Roscommon*'s excellent *Essay on Translated Verse*: Which, I think, is proper to stand in This Place, both as a Conclusion of my Preface, and as a Kind of Poetical Invocation to my Work:

Hail mighty MARO! *May That sacred Name*
Kindle my Breast with Thy celestial Flame;
Sublime Ideas, and apt Words infuse:
The Muse instruct my Voice, and THOU *inspire the Muse.*

FOOTNOTES:

[1] *Prælectiones Poeticæ.*

[2] *Merchant of Venice.*

[3] *De tous les Ouvrages dont l'Esprit de l'Homme est capable, le Poem Epique est sans doute le plus accompli.*

[4] *For so it should certainly be read; tho' both in the Folio and Octavo Editions, 'tis* Aristotle.

[5] *Preface to his Fables.*

[6] Elogia Virgilii Cap. IV Major *Homero.*

[7] *The Word was originally applied to Dramatic Poetry, and from thence transferred to Epic.* Aristotle *uses it in more Senses than one; which seem not to be rightly distinguished by his Interpreters. However we are for that Reason more at Liberty to apply it, as we think most proper.*

[8] *For he mentions several Episodes, which he allows to be truly such; which yet are only convenient, not necessary. And besides, he says, p. 100, and in other Places,* Une Episode est une partie necessaire de l'Action: *And yet, p. 102,* Le premier plan de l'Action contient *seulement ce qui est propre & necessaire* à la Fable; &

n'a aucune Episode. By *which he* seems at least *to allow that an Episode may not be necessary.*

[9] Τὸ μὲν οὖν ἴδιον τοῦτο, τὰ δ' ἄλλα ἐπεισόδια. Poetic. Cap XVII.

[10] *The one is* ☐διον, *the other is o*☐*κε*☐*ον. The former is of a more* close, restrained, *and* peculiar *Signification, than the latter: The former relating* most properly *to a Man*'s Person; *the latter to his* Possessions.

[11] *Preface to* Homer.

[12] *Dedication of the Æneis.*

[13] *See* Bossu, *Chap. IX.*

[14] *Upon the Article of* Virgil's *Invention, see* M. Segrais *at large in his admirable Preface to his Translation of the Æneis; and from him Mr.* Dryden *in his Dedication of the Æneis, p. 226,* &c. *of the Folio Edition.*

[15] *Preface* to Juvenal.

[16] Paradise lost, *Book VII.*

[17] *Preface to Mr.* Pope's Homer.

[18] P. 142. *Second Edition.*

[19] *P. 158.*

[20] *Præl. Poet.* Vol. I. Præl. 2.

[21] *Verses before* L. Roscommon's *Essay. And Preface to his* Virgil.

[22] *Preface to it.*

[23] Dr. Swift *in his Letter to the Earl of* Oxford.

[24] *Preface to his* Virgil.

Milton Keynes UK
Ingram Content Group UK Ltd.
UKHW050242220624
444555UK00005BA/484